The SPACE *Between* Replies

Emily Elizabeth Hickman

Title: The SPACE Between Replies
Author: Emily Elizabeth Hickman

Published by Pine Tree Press

www.pinetreepress.com

Printed in USA

This book is dedicated to my *children*

and Eric.

You make my life better.

CONTENTS

Author's Note: Why This Book Exists....................................1

How to Use This Book 1

1. Read the Story First....................................1

2. Check Your Initial "Vibe" 1

3. Read Between the Lines 1

4. Make Your Guess....................................1

5. Sit with the Reveal 2

6. Reflect (Only If You Want To) 2

P A R T I : 1

The Four Attachment Styles....................................1

Solo Attachment Patterns 1

The Mission 2

Chapter 1:....................................1

LOW BATTERY WARNING 1

Chapter 2: 1

PHANTOM VIBRATION....................................1

Chapter 3: 1

AIRPLANE MODE....................................1

Chapter 4: 1

UNSTABLE CONNECTION....................................1

P A R T I I : 1

When Attachment Styles Collide 1
Combined & Relational Patterns 1
The Mission: 2
Chapter 5: 1
SIGNAL LOSS 1
Chapter 6: 1
FULL SIGNAL, NO CONNECTION 1
Chapter 7: 1
UNREAD 1
Chapter 8: 1
DELIVERED 1
Part III: 1
You Are Not One Thing 1
Integration & Evolution 1
The Mission: 2
Chapter 9: 1
SIGNAL AND STRENGTH 1
Chapter 10: 1
HARD RESET: MOVING BEYOND FACTORY SETTINGS 1
Chapter 10 Worksheet 6
CH 11: 1
OVERRIDE THE DEFAULTS 1

P A R T I V : *Closing*....................................1
CH 12:....................................1
PERSONALIZING THE SETTINGS 1

Author's Note: Why This Book Exists

We've all been there: staring at a text we can't stop overthinking. Walking away from something good when we should have stayed. Staying in something bad when we should have run.

In those moments, it's easy to feel like you're the problem. Like you're "bad at love," too sensitive, or just broken.

But you're not.

Humans are wired for connection. We aren't born knowing how to do it perfectly. We learn how to attach to others based on our past experiences—the good, the bad, and the silent. Our nervous systems learned how to protect us, and they carry those lessons into every new relationship, often on autopilot.

This book exists to turn that autopilot into something you can see.

The stories inside are designed to be a mirror, not a diagnosis. They are portraits of the four main attachment patterns you'll find in the world (and maybe in yourself). There's no judgment here. There's no "right" or "wrong" way to feel; there is only your way.

My goal isn't to put you in a box with a label on it. It's to help you recognize these patterns without shame. When you see your own story reflected in these pages, the chaos can start to feel less personal and more universal.

So, read the stories. Don't overthink the quizzes at the end. Your heart knows the answers already; you just have to give it a moment to speak.

We're all just trying to figure out how to be safe and connected at the same time.

Welcome to the journey.

How to Use This Book

This isn't a textbook. Think of it as an interactive mirror. Here is how to navigate these stories in a way that makes it easier for you:

1. Read the Story First

Try to get lost in the world. Don't look for clinical markers right away—just feel the character's reality. Notice the "digital body language" on their screen, the way they breathe, and the choices they make when things get real.

2. Check Your Initial "Vibe"

After each story, you'll find a First Impression Check. This is for your nervous system. Before you analyze the psychology, take a second to notice how the ending actually made you feel. Were you relieved? Stressed? Proud? There are no wrong answers.

3. Read Between the Lines

The Reflection Questions are designed to help you spot the invisible patterns. Attachment isn't always about big blowouts; usually, it's in the quiet things—the way a text is phrased or the reason someone chooses a specific seat in a restaurant.

4. Make Your Guess

Once you've sat with the story, it's time to play detective. Use the Guess the Attachment Style section to see if you can name the pattern. This isn't about being "right"—it's about training your brain to recognize these behaviors in the wild.

5. *Sit with the Reveal*

After the guess, you'll find The Reveal and a Real Talk Moment. This is where we break down the "why" behind the behavior. It's a chance to see how that specific style protects itself and how it connects with others.

6. *Reflect (Only If You Want To)*

The Quick Self-Reflect at the end is a space for you. You don't have to write anything down if you don't want to. It's just an invitation to see if any part of that character's heart looks like yours.

You can go in order, or you can skip around. This is your journey. Use it however it helps you feel more seen.

PART I:

The Four Attachment Styles

Solo Attachment Patterns

Every text sent, every "read" receipt ignored, and every late-night "Are you up?" is a signal.

We often think attachment only happens when we are with someone. But the truth is, our attachment style is often most visible in the quiet moments — the space between the Sent and the Reply. It is the internal map we use to navigate uncertainty when we are alone with our thoughts... and our phones.

These four stories are portraits of the primary ways our hearts learned to survive. As you read, your goal is to decode the "glitch" or the "grounding" in each one before the reveal.

THE MISSION

As you read, look for these three clues:

The Internal Monologue

Is it a war zone, a quiet room, or a shifting floor?

The Phone

Is it a tool, a weapon, or an alarm system?

The Goal

Are they seeking safety, space, or connection?

Don't look for an answer.

Look for a pattern.

Chapter 1:

LOW BATTERY WARNING

I don’t count the minutes, but notice the light change in the room, sinking down the walls. The way afternoon thins into something flatter, more metallic, the light losing its warmth.

I drink the water I just poured and refill the glass without realizing it’s already full. It spills over the rim, quiet and sudden, pooling against my palm. I don't scramble for a towel; I just watch the way it catches the light on my skin before wiping my hand on my jeans. It’s just water. It’ll dry.

My phone vibrates against the counter.

Yeah, he writes. *That could be nice.*

It’s the kind of message that used to send me into a spiral of "what ifs." Now, it just looked like a low battery warning: a notification of something fading out, but not a crisis.

I don’t reply right away. Instead, I open the window above the sink. The air outside carries a faint scent of rain, though the sky is still clear. Somewhere nearby, a train horn blows—a low, steady pulse. It doesn't sound lonely to me anymore; it just sounds like something moving exactly where it's supposed to go. I finish my water, watch a bird land on the fence for a second, and then type back.

A version of myself surfaces: the one who used to decode his language like scripture. Who could tell the difference between *yeah* and *sure* and *maybe later*. Who lived inside the pauses between his words, convinced meaning hid there. I don't live there anymore.

Still, something in the message catches me, not fear exactly, but recognition. A kind of sense memory. Like brushing a scar you forgot about because it no longer hurts.

I type back, still standing at the sink.

I'm free Thursday evening. Let me know.

This time, I set the phone on the counter and look out the window.

The waiting shifts. It's not about him, it's about what showing up would mean. How proximity rearranges memory. How easily old roles slip back into place, like ghosts reclaiming their favorite chairs.

Outside, a car door slams. Someone laughs a few houses down. A dog barks once and then stops. The light fades with a strange hesitation, like a stage being reset while the audience is still watching.

When my phone buzzes again, I don't flinch.

That night, I dreamed of a hallway with too many doors. Every handle is warm. Every room sounds occupied.

I wake before I open any of them.

Thursday arrives without ceremony.

I don't dress for nostalgia. I wear what I always wear when I want to feel like myself—soft fabric, dark boots. I catch my reflection in the mirror and notice how ordinary I look. Solid. I feel a quiet sense of readiness that feels earned.

His message comes an hour before we were supposed to meet.

Does the old place still do that soup you like?

My stomach tightens, just slightly. The old place. The soup. A memory offered like proof of intimacy.

I study the message. The way it reaches backward without acknowledging distance. The way it assumes access.

I type slowly. *They do. I'll meet you there at seven.*

The restaurant hasn't changed. Same chipped mugs. Same uneven tables. The same mirror behind the bar that makes the room look deeper than it is. I arrive first. I choose a table by the window because I want to watch the rain.

The waitress smiles at me as if I'm a regular. I'm not—I haven't been back since the last time I sat across from him.

When he walks in, I recognize him instantly. And then I recognize him again, the way you recognize a scar you'd almost forgotten was there.

He looks mostly the same. Familiar face. Familiar posture. But there's something else now, something watchful in his eyes. Like he's scanning for where he fits.

We hug, briefly. His arms linger a second too long. I step back before it becomes a thing.

"You look good," he says.

"So do you," I reply, because it's true and because it doesn't cost me anything to say it.

We sit. The table is narrow enough that our knees almost touch.

Conversation settles into the grooves it remembers. Work. Travel. People we both know but no longer talk to. He laughs at the same places. I notice how often he steers the topic back to us without naming it.

I drink from a glass with a crack in it, my thumb tracing the ridge. I've always known how to navigate things that are broken. Like an extra sense.

At one point, he says, "I always wondered if we'd run into each other again like this."

"Like what?" I ask.

He pauses. Smiles. "Like nothing happened."

The words land heavier than he seems to intend.

I set my spoon down carefully.

“That’s not how it feels to me,” I say.

The space between us tightens. Not hostile. Alert.

He watches me like I’ve changed the rules mid-game.

“Oh,” he says. “I didn’t mean...”

“I know,” I say. And I do. He means comfort. Familiarity. A version of the past that doesn’t ask anything of him.

I let the silence stretch. It doesn’t scare me. It does something else—it clarifies.

Outside, the sky finally breaks. Rain streaks the window in thin, vertical lines, distorting the streetlights into long, trembling shapes. The world looks warped but contained, like it’s being held behind glass.

He leans forward, lowering his voice. “I missed this. You. The way things were.”

There it is. Not a confession. An offering.

I feel the old gravity tug once—soft, insistent. I feel how easy it would be to step back into his orbit. To be familiar. To be wanted in a way that doesn’t require conquering new ground.

I don’t.

“I didn’t,” I say, gently. “Not like that.”

I continue, "I remember the way we were, but I've grown into a different version of myself now. I'm okay with where we are today. I can see why you'd feel that way, it was a very comfortable time. But I'm enjoying the person I am now much more."

Something flickers across his face. Surprise. Then something closer to resentment, quickly masked.

"Oh," he says again. This time it's different. Sharper. Like a door clicking shut.

I realize then what the unease has been circling: not the fear of being pulled back but the awareness that he thought he still could. The power shift is quiet. Almost invisible.

When we stand to leave, the rain has slowed to a mist. We hesitate on the sidewalk, the space between us charged but undefined.

"Well," he says, his hands shoved deep in his pockets. "It was good seeing you."

"It was," I agree.

We don't hug this time.

I offer a final, easy smile before turning toward my street. I walk away, my pace steady, feeling the night closing behind me like something finished but not sealed.

Half a block later, my phone vibrates.

I stop under a streetlight and turn it over. The rain mist settling over the screen.

You've changed, he writes.

I consider the sentence. The accusation hiding inside it. The nostalgia trying to dress itself up as loss.

I reply, *I have. It's a good thing. Take care.*

I slip the phone back into my pocket and keep walking.

FIRST IMPRESSION CHECK

Be honest. No overthinking.

When the story ended, I felt:

☐ relieved

☐ uneasy

☐ calm

☐ curious

☐ low-key stressed

☐ kind of proud of her

☐ not sure yet

Which moment stuck with you the most?

(There's no right answer. Your nervous system noticed what it noticed.)

READ BETWEEN THE LINES

Sometimes what matters most is what isn't said.

Which of these felt true in the story?

☐ She trusted herself more than she trusted the situation

☐ He assumed they were picking up where they left off

☐ The tension was quiet, not dramatic

☐ Nothing "bad" happened, but something important did

Anything else you noticed?

WHAT WOULD YOU HAVE DONE?

No judgment. Just curiosity.

If you were in her place, would you have:

☐ replied faster

☐ tried to keep things light

☐ asked what he really meant

☐ avoided meeting up at all

☐ handled it the same way

What choice feels most like you?

OKAY, TIME FOR THE GUESS

If you had to guess, which attachment style do you think the main character shows?

☐ Secure

☐ Anxious

☐ Avoidant

☐ Fearful-Avoidant

☐ I have no idea but I'm vibing

Hold that thought...

THE REVEAL

This story reflects a Secure Attachment pattern.

That usually looks like:

- being okay with closeness and space
- not chasing reassurance
- not pulling away to stay safe
- trusting your own feelings instead of trying to control someone else's

Secure doesn't mean unbothered.

It means she didn't abandon herself to keep the connection.

REAL TALK MOMENT

Secure attachment often comes from:

- having someone consistent early on
- learning boundaries later in life
- therapy, healing, or just getting tired of chaos
- doing the work to build an 'Earned' sense of safety

It is not about being cooler, stronger, or more lovable.

It's about feeling safe enough to be honest.

QUICK SELF-REFLECT (NO PRESSURE)

When someone I care about feels distant, I usually:

☐ try harder

☐ act like I don't care

☐ overthink everything

☐ wait and see

☐ distract myself

What do I usually need most in those moments?

LAST THOUGHT BEFORE THE NEXT STORY

The way you react in relationships makes sense once you understand what your heart learned to expect.

Next story, you'll meet someone whose heart learned something very different.

Chapter 2:

PHANTOM VIBRATION

We spent the whole day together, it was good. Actually, not good; great!

Not movie-perfect. Better than that. Easy. Comfortable. The kind of day where everything feels like it's quietly clicking into place. He held my hand when we crossed the street, and for those few blocks, I felt like I was finally being translated into a language I actually spoke. I didn't just like him, I thought he was wonderful; I felt made of glass and sunlight; fluid and sparkly.

At one point, sitting on the edge of the fountain, he leaned in and said, "I like you like this," as if he'd just discovered a new color. The stone was gritty and sun-warmed under my palms, and the air smelled like old pennies and chlorine. The water spray was a fine, cool mist against my neck. I told myself not to memorize the sound of his voice when he said it. I did anyway.

When he dropped me off, he kissed me slow and soft. “I’ll text you later,” he said.

I believed him.

At home, I left my jacket on the back of the chair because it still smelled like him. I didn’t even change my clothes. I replayed little pieces of the day while my phone sat on the bed, its screen casting a pale, digital blue against the ceiling. I felt an electric hum in my chest, a dizzying euphoria I wanted to bottle up.

I didn’t count the minutes, but I noticed the way the afternoon sun turned a bruised peach color, bleeding across the floorboards until the shadows of the furniture looked longer and sharper than the objects themselves.

Two hours passed.

I opened my phone, then closed it. I checked my own profile to see what I looked like through his eyes. I was ghost-hunting in my own life. I checked his story. No new posts. I wondered if he was okay. I wondered if he was staring at his ceiling, thinking about the fountain, or if he had already moved on to the next part of his night where I didn't exist.

The floor felt like it was shifting just enough to make me dizzy. My bedroom felt too quiet, like a held breath. I didn't want to be the girl who turns a good day into a problem, so I tried to be "pro-relationship." I tried to care for the connection.

I sent a picture I'd taken of the fountain earlier. *Found another coin in my pocket,* I wrote. *Should I go back and make a wish for us, or are we good for now?*

I held my breath. I wasn't asking for much, just a tiny signal that the "us" was still real.

The message delivered instantly. No reply.

This is the part I hate, the part where my brain starts auditioning explanations. I tried to watch a video, but the words were white noise. I lasted six minutes before checking the thread again. I looked at his last message from earlier—the one with the heart at the end. I used it as a buoy to keep from sinking.

Trust that good things don't disappear just because they pause, I whispered to myself.

My phone buzzed. My heart jumped so hard it actually hurt. It was a notification for a sale at a store I don't even like. I stared at the screen, embarrassed by how much that little vibration took out of me.

Finally, his name lit up the screen.

Sorry, he wrote. *Got caught up. But yeah, today was nice.*

Nice. Nice is a placeholder. It's what you say about a weather report. It wasn't the word I had spent the last three hours building a shrine for. A small, bitter wall rose up in me—a need to protect myself. He took three hours; I gave him forty minutes of my own silence. A tiny, invisible test to see if he'd try to climb over it.

When I finally replied, I made sure my *Yeah* sounded as casual as his *Nice.*

But my chest still felt tight. I wanted to be the person who needed less, but I was tired of pretending. I wanted to know if the ground was still solid.

I sent another text, masked as a joke: *You're being awfully quiet. Should I be worried that I laughed too loud at your jokes today, or are you just playing it cool?*

The dots appeared immediately. Then disappeared. Then appeared again.

Neither, he wrote. *I just take things slow.*

Slow. Slow to him was a safety rail. Slow to me felt like a long, slow-motion fall.

I get that, I replied. *I just didn't want to overthink. I like where this is going.*

You don't have to overthink, he responded. *Me too.*

I exhaled, a wave of relief washing over me—warm and dizzying. And still... something underneath it stayed alert. I added a smiley face to my next text and left it there, a tiny peace offering.

I set my phone down, but I kept the ringer on high. I did feel good. Mostly. But part of me was already trying to memorize the way this relief felt, just in case the quiet came back tomorrow. That part of me doesn't trust the calm unless it keeps proving itself.

I told myself I didn't need to solve the future tonight. I closed my eyes, but I kept my phone tucked under my pillow, the vibration motor resting against my ear. I fell asleep waiting for a sound that hadn't happened yet.

<u>FIRST IMPRESSION CHECK</u>

No thinking too hard. Just what your body noticed.

When the story ended, I felt:

☐ relieved

☐ hopeful

☐ still kind of nervous

☐ happy for her

☐ tense the whole time

☐ seen (in an uncomfortable way)

☐ not sure yet

What part of the story stayed with you most?

<u>READ BETWEEN THE LINES</u>

Sometimes it's not about what happens.

It's about what we do when we don't know what's happening.

Which of these showed up in the story?

☐ replaying moments to check if they meant something

☐ watching the phone more than the room

☐ wanting reassurance but not wanting to ask

☐ feeling calm only after getting a response

☐ trying to stay "cool" while feeling anything but

Anything else you noticed?

WHAT WOULD YOU HAVE DONE?

Be honest. Be kind to yourself.

If you were in her place, would you have:

☐ texted first

☐ waited longer

☐ asked for clarity

☐ pretended you weren't bothered

☐ handled it the same way

Which choice feels most like you?

TIME TO GUESS (JUST FOR FUN)

If you had to guess, which attachment pattern do you think this story shows?

☐ Secure

☐ Anxious

☐ Avoidant

☐ Fearful-Avoidant

☐ I have no idea but I felt it

Hold that thought...

THE REVEAL

This story reflects an Anxious Attachment pattern.

This often looks like:

- needing reassurance to feel calm
- worrying when things feel uncertain
- feeling very connected very quickly
- noticing small changes in tone or timing

Anxious attachment doesn't mean "too much."

It usually means your heart learned that connection can disappear without warning.

So it stays alert.

REAL TALK MOMENT

People with anxious attachment often care deeply, love intensely, and notice emotional shifts that others miss.

That's not weakness.

That's sensitivity shaped by experience.

The hard part is when your nervous system starts working overtime trying to keep someone close.

QUICK SELF-REFLECT

When I start to feel unsure about someone, I usually:

☐ want to talk it out immediately

☐ overthink everything they say or don't say

☐ blame myself

☐ distract myself

☐ act like I don't care

What usually helps me feel better?

What usually makes it worse?

LAST THOUGHT BEFORE THE NEXT STORY

Wanting closeness doesn't make you needy.

It means connection matters to you.

Next, you'll meet someone who wants connection too —

Chapter 3:

AIRPLANE MODE

We've been seeing each other for three months, which feels like the exact right amount of time to enjoy the heat of a fire without worrying about the structure of the house. Three months is long enough to know that his coffee order is a double-shot with a ridiculous amount of sugar. Long enough that my spare toothbrush has a permanent home in his bathroom cabinet, and his gray hoodie has become the unofficial upholstery of my passenger seat.

I like him. That part is easy. He has a way of looking at me like I'm the only thing in the room worth paying attention to, and for a while, I let myself live in that light. But lately, I've noticed the way time keeps moving forward, dragging expectations behind it like a heavy, velvet tail.

We're walking back from dinner on a Tuesday night. The air is thick and syrupy, the sidewalk still radiating the day's heat through the soles of my boots. Cars pass with their windows down, the bass from their speakers thudding against my ribs before breaking into pieces as they fade into the distance.

He reaches for my hand. I let him. Our fingers fit together perfectly—a seamless, warm lock—but I tell myself it doesn't have to mean anything more than what it is. I focus on the rhythm of our footsteps on the concrete, trying to keep my thoughts as flat as the pavement.

"Can I ask you something?" he says.

My stomach tightens before I even know why. It's a physical reaction, a silent alarm bell ringing in a room I thought was empty. I don't look at him. Instead, I watch the numbers on the crosswalk sign across the street. It blinks a harsh, neon red, counting down the seconds we have left to stand still. 10. 9. 8.

"Where do you see this going?"

There it is. Not dramatic. Not an ultimatum. Just a direct, honest question.

I keep my eyes on the street ahead, where the asphalt looks like a river of oil under the yellow streetlamps. "I don't know," I say, and my voice sounds remarkably flat, even to me. "I'm just kind of taking things as they come."

He nods, filing the answer away. I can feel him wanting to reach for more, but I've already stepped back mentally. The "us" of the situation is starting to feel like a heavy winter coat in the middle of July. I just want to stand up straight. I want to be able to breathe without feeling like I'm inhaling someone else's air.

"I just don't want to rush into something and then regret it," I add, my voice taking on a logical, reasonable edge. It's my favorite shield.

He stops walking then, right under the buzzing hum of a streetlight. "Do you think you would regret being with me?"

The question lands softly, but it feels like a snare. "No," I say quickly, and I mean it. He's wonderful. But what I can't say is: I don't want to wake up one day and feel trapped by a version of myself I agreed to be for you. I don't want to be a piece of a set. I want to stay a whole, separate thing.

We reach my car. The silence between us is a different kind of heavy now, not the comfortable kind we had on the couch, but something dense and pressurized. He leans in to hug me, and I wrap my arms around him automatically. He smells like woodsmoke and the expensive detergent his mom buys, a scent that is becoming dangerously familiar. I notice how easy it would be to just stay there, to let the weight of him anchor me.

I let go first. I step back into the cool, air-conditioned safety of my car, feeling the space between us return like a physical shield. It's a relief that tastes like ozone before a storm.

After that night, things don't exactly change, which is the most unsettling part. He still texts me in the mornings. He still invites me over when he's made too much pasta. I still go. We still laugh at the same inside jokes, the ones that have built a small, private language between us.

If anyone asked, I'd say everything is fine. And it is. Mostly. But there's a new, quiet awareness in the room. I see it in the way he lingers a second too long after a kiss, or how he looks at me when he thinks I'm not paying attention—like he's waiting for a door to open that I've quietly deadbolted.

One night, we're lying on his bed, staring at the ceiling fan as it slices the shadows into repetitive, rhythmic blades. The room is dim, lit only by the blue glow of a salt lamp in the corner.

"I told my sister about you today," he says quietly. "She asked if you were my girlfriend."

The word feels like a physical weight dropping onto my chest. I sit up abruptly, swinging my legs off the bed so I can feel the cold hardwood floor beneath my feet. It grounds me. I don't want to sign a contract I haven't read yet. To me, labels aren't just words; they are expectations. They are debts I'm not sure I want to owe.

"I don't want to mess this up," I say, looking at my hands in the dark. "I just think labels change things. I need to take things at my own pace."

He exhales slowly, a long, weary sound that makes the air in the room feel thin. "Okay," he says. "I can do that."

But something shifts. The urgency in him begins to go dormant. He stops bringing up the future. He stops looking at me like I'm a puzzle he's desperate to solve. And part of me—the loudest part—feels an immense, cooling relief.

A few weeks later, he tells me he's moving across town to live with his cousin. "It's closer to work," he explains, his voice casual, almost detached.

"That's cool," I say. "Makes total sense."

As I watch him pack a small box of kitchen supplies, I feel a physical loosening in my chest, the distinct click of a lock turning. It isn't that I want him gone; I just want the pressure of being "the one" to stop leaning on me. When he moves, the relationship gets quieter. We see each other once a week instead of three. We text in short, functional bursts.

I tell myself that this is what healthy looks like. Comfortable. Uncomplicated. A relationship that lives in the margins of my life instead of taking up the whole page.

The final text comes weeks later, on a Tuesday when the sky is a bruised, ink-wash purple. My phone vibrates on the nightstand, a sharp, solitary sound in the empty room.

I met someone today, he writes. *I think I might actually like her.*

I stare at the message until the blue light of the screen begins to burn my eyes. My brain does that thing it's best at: it files the "us" folder away and clicks the drawer shut. I feel a brief, cold sting in my throat, but it's quickly followed by a flood of quiet. The weight is finally, completely off my shoulders. I don't have to wonder if I'm giving enough anymore. The debt is settled.

I'm happy for you, I type back. I mean it. Mostly.

I set the phone down and look around my apartment. It is perfectly quiet. Perfectly empty. Everything is exactly where I put it. There are no spare toothbrushes in the sink that aren't mine. There are no hoodies on the chairs.

I stayed in control. I stayed safe. I kept the walls up and the doors locked, and I didn't let anyone trip the alarms.

But as I lie back in the silence, I realize that safety feels a lot like distance. I chose the space, and I got exactly what I wanted. I just didn't expect the air in the room to feel so cold once I was the only one left to breathe it. I was the one who stepped back first, and now, I'm the only one left in the room.

FIRST IMPRESSION CHECK

No overthinking. Just what you felt.

When the story ended, I felt:

☐ calm but kind of sad

☐ frustrated with her

☐ like I understood her

☐ relieved nothing "blew up"

☐ low-key emotional

☐ confused about how I feel

☐ not sure yet

What part of the story stuck with you most?

READ BETWEEN THE LINES

Sometimes people don't leave because they don't care.

Sometimes they leave because they care too much to feel safe.

Which of these showed up in the story?

☐ changing the subject when things got emotional

☐ avoiding labels even when feelings were there

☐ wanting closeness but not wanting expectations

☐ feeling relieved when distance happened

☐ saying "I'm fine" and mostly meaning it

Anything else you noticed?

WHAT WOULD YOU HAVE DONE?

No right answers. Just you.

If you were in her place, would you have:

☐ defined the relationship

☐ stayed quiet like she did

☐ ended things earlier

☐ tried to keep it casual

☐ asked what he really wanted

Which choice feels most like you?

TIME TO GUESS (JUST FOR FUN)

Which attachment pattern do you think this story reflects?

☐ Secure

☐ Anxious

☐ Avoidant

☐ Fearful-Avoidant

☐ I don’t know, but it felt familiar

Hold that thought...

THE REVEAL

This story reflects an Avoidant Attachment pattern.

This often looks like:

- liking someone but keeping emotional space
- feeling uncomfortable when things get serious
- valuing independence a lot
- pulling back when expectations appear

Avoidant attachment doesn't mean someone doesn't care.

It usually means closeness feels risky, even when it's wanted.

REAL TALK MOMENT

People with avoidant attachment are often:

- independent
- reliable
- calm in conflict
- good at handling things on their own

The hard part is letting someone see the softer parts that feel harder to protect.

Sometimes distance feels safer than being wanted.

QUICK SELF-REFLECT

When someone gets emotionally close to me, I usually:

☐ feel uncomfortable

☐ change the subject

☐ want more space

☐ overthink everything

☐ secretly want closeness but don't show it

What feels hardest about letting someone really know me?

What helps me feel safer with people?

LAST THOUGHT BEFORE THE NEXT STORY

Wanting independence doesn't mean you don't want love.

It just means your heart learned to stay safe by standing alone.

Next, you'll meet someone whose heart wants closeness —

Chapter 4:

UNSTABLE CONNECTION

We always say we're done like we mean it. We use final, heavy words that feel like slamming a vault door shut. Block. Delete. I've written long, bruising speeches about how this isn't healthy, how we are a house built on a fault line. I've sent those texts with a trembling thumb, then stared at my reflection in the dark screen until I looked like a stranger to myself. I've deleted his number, wiped our thread, and told my roommate to hide my phone if I so much as mention his name.

Then something small happens. A song with a specific bassline. A memory of a Tuesday night when the air smelled exactly like this, cool and heavy with the promise of rain. The quiet in my apartment begins to feel louder than it should, a pressing, physical weight against my eardrums. I find myself ghost-hunting, looking for his shadow in the corner of the room, listening for a laugh that isn't there.

And suddenly we're back in each other's orbit, pretending the gravity isn't intentional.

This time, it starts with a vibration that rattles the glass of water on my nightstand. I don't even have to look. I know the rhythm of the buzz.

Are you up?

Three words I know better than my own name. I stare at the screen for a full minute, the blue light bleaching the color from my duvet cover. I know this road. I know the exact curve where we always lose control, and yet, my fingers move on their own.

Yeah.

I tell myself I'm calm. I tell myself I can handle a conversation without catching fire. Five minutes later, his car pulls up to the curb. The hallway light outside my door is flickering—a jagged, nervous strobe that matches the frantic pulse in my throat. When I open the door, he looks like a ghost I haven't finished mourning. He smells like the same cedarwood soap he's always used, a scent that hits me like a physical blow. I hate that my body relaxes the second I see him, the tension in my shoulders finally unspooling like a broken thread.

"I wasn't trying to mess with your head," he says, his voice low and raspy. He steps into the dim warmth of my apartment, and the air between us suddenly feels pressurized, like we're in a plane that's losing altitude. "I just... I missed you."

My chest tightens, a sharp, familiar ache. "That's how it always starts," I say, but I don't ask him to leave. I don't even move.

We sit on the couch, but we don't sit close. There is a "readerly gap" of exactly twelve inches between us. We talk about work, about my roommate's new cat, about the rain that still hasn't quite started. We laugh at the same dumb jokes, but the laughter is thin, a paper-thin bridge over a dark canyon. His hand finds mine on the cushion, lacing our fingers together with a terrifying, effortless muscle memory. The grit of his palm against mine feels more real than anything I've felt in weeks.

"I don't want to hurt you again," he says quietly, staring at our joined hands.

The words again, they land like a stone in a well. I should hear it as honesty. Instead, I hear it as a countdown. My heart does that familiar flip—the one that feels like falling and bracing at the same time.

"Then don't," I say, but my voice is a whisper.

He looks at me, his eyes searching mine for a map he lost a long time ago. "I just don't know how to do this without messing it up," he says.

The second he says those words, the internal alarm in my blood goes off. It's too loud to ignore. I pull my hand away, my skin suddenly feeling too hot, too exposed. I need to touch something cold, something that isn't him. I scramble off the couch and stand by the window, pressing my forehead against the glass.

"See, this is what I mean," I say, my breath fogging the pane. "You show up, you say these things, and then when it gets real, you don’t actually want anything. You're just checking to see if I'm still here.”

“That’s not fair,” he says, his jaw tightening as he stands up.

“Isn’t it? Every time we get close, you pull back. And I’m left standing on the platform watching the train leave. I feel like I’m waiting for you to disappear, so yeah, maybe I don’t make it easy. Maybe I start the fire before you can leave me in the cold.”

He runs a hand through his hair, a gesture of pure exhaustion. “I’m trying,” he says. “But every time I try to give you space, you pull me back. And every time I stay, you freak out and push me away.”

He’s right. The second I feel how much I want him to stay, fear hits me like a bucket of ice water. Wanting that much feels like giving him a loaded gun and hoping he won't pull the trigger.

The silence between us is thick and uncomfortable, until he finally says, “Can we just... sit for a minute? No talking. Just sitting.”

I nod, even though I don’t trust my own skin. We sit back down, further apart this time. The only sound is the hum of the fridge and the distant, muffled roar of a car on the wet street outside. I can feel the heat radiating from his leg, a magnetic pull I have to fight to ignore.

“I don’t want to lose you,” he says. “Even when we’re bad at this.”

That is the crack in my armor. My chest aches, a sharp, physical pain that makes it hard to breathe. "I don't want to lose you either," I admit. "I just don't know how to trust that you won't leave."

He turns toward me, hesitates, then touches my cheek like he's afraid I might flinch. I don't. I lean into his hand, and that's all it takes. We kiss like people who have been holding their breath underwater—urgent, familiar, way too easy. My hands grip his shirt, the fabric bunching under my knuckles, like I'm afraid he might vanish if I let go.

For a moment, it's simple. The world is just the taste of him and the sound of our breathing. "Stay," I whisper.

He goes quiet. He doesn't pull away, but he doesn't answer either. The pause stretches, and I feel the shift, that subtle, cold change in the air right before the drop. My heart starts doing that stupid, hopeful thing, and I hate it. I hate it because I know what comes next.

"I want to," he says slowly. "I just... I don't want us to hurt each other again."

The hope in my chest twists into something sharp and jagged. I stand up, my hands shaking even though I'm trying to keep them flat against my sides. "So what, this is just temporary? Again? You want me, just not enough to actually choose me."

"That's not fair," he says. "I'm being honest."

"And I'm tired of half-answers," I snap. "I'm tired of being the one who feels more."

His face closes off, the light in his eyes going out like a blown fuse. "I never asked you to feel more," he says quietly.

The words hit me like a punch to the stomach. I stand by the door, the hallway light still flickering behind me, casting long, jittery shadows. "Then maybe we should stop. Because I can't keep pretending this doesn't mess with me."

He looks at me, and for the first time, he doesn't look like he's going to fight. He just looks tired. "I don't think we know how to do this without hurting each other," he says.

"Maybe we're just bad at timing," I whisper.

"Or bad at letting go," he says.

At the door, he hesitates, his hand on the cold brass handle. "I really do love you," he says.

"I love you too," I say, because lying would feel worse than just stating the truth.

For a split second, I think he might turn around. I think we'll collapse into each other and undo every word we just said. He doesn't. The door closes, a soft but definite click that echoes in the empty hallway.

I stand there listening to his footsteps fade, my chest aching with things I didn't protect myself from after all. I tell myself this is for the best. That love isn't supposed to feel like a war between your heart and your mind. But later, I still check my phone, half-hoping for a buzz, half-dreading it.

I lay in bed staring at the jittery shadows on the ceiling—missing him and relieved he's gone, wanting him back and knowing I can't trust what happens if he comes. Loving someone shouldn't feel like this, but for me, it always has. And as I drift off, I'm still waiting for a sound that hasn't happened yet.

FIRST IMPRESSION CHECK

No thinking too hard. Just what you felt.

When the story ended, I felt:

☐ emotional

☐ frustrated for both of them

☐ sad but not surprised

☐ like yelling "just stay!"

☐ exhausted for her

☐ weirdly understood

☐ not sure yet

What moment hit you the hardest?

READ BETWEEN THE LINES

Sometimes people want closeness and fear it at the same time.

Which of these showed up in the story?

☐ pulling someone close, then pushing them away

☐ feeling safest when someone leaves — and loneliest after

☐ needing reassurance but not trusting it

☐ expecting things to fall apart

☐ wanting love but bracing for loss

Anything else you noticed?

WHAT WOULD YOU HAVE DONE?

No judgment. This one is complicated.

If you were in her place, would you have:

☐ stayed and tried again

☐ ended things earlier

☐ asked for clearer commitment

☐ pulled away like she did

☐ gone back after he left

Which choice feels most like you?

<u>TIME TO GUESS (JUST FOR FUN)</u>

Which attachment pattern do you think this story reflects?

☐ Secure

☐ Anxious

☐ Avoidant

☐ Fearful-Avoidant

☐ I don't know but it felt intense

Hold that thought...

THE REVEAL

This story reflects a Fearful-Avoidant Attachment pattern.

This often looks like:

- wanting closeness very badly
- feeling unsafe when it actually happens
- pulling someone in, then pushing them away
- expecting relationships to end even when love is real

It's not that they don't want love.

It's that love feels risky.

So their heart stays in defense mode.

REAL TALK MOMENT

People with fearful-avoidant attachment often:

- feel deeply
- love intensely
- notice emotional shifts fast
- and protect themselves hard

They want connection.

They just don't trust that it won't hurt.

So they live in that space between come closer and don't leave me—and, I don't need you.

And that's exhausting.

QUICK SELF-REFLECT

When I start to care about someone, I usually:

☐ get very close very fast

☐ start worrying they'll leave

☐ pull away to protect myself

☐ test how much they care

☐ feel torn between wanting them and wanting space

What scares me most about relationships?

What makes me feel emotionally safe with someone?

LAST THOUGHT BEFORE WHAT COMES NEXT

Wanting love and fearing it at the same time doesn't mean you're broken.

It means your heart learned that closeness can hurt and it's trying to keep you safe.

Next, we'll look at how attachment can shift, mix, and change because most people don't fit into just one pattern.

PART II:

When Attachment Styles Collide

Combined & Relational Patterns

If Part I was about the internal map, Part II is about the collision.

Attachment isn't just something that lives inside you; it's something that happens *between* people. It's what happens when a "low battery" meets an "over-charged" heart, or when two people are both waiting for the other to drop the shield first.

In this section, we move beyond individual portraits and into the dynamics. This isn't about labeling people as "the problem"—it's about recognizing the dance that happens when two different survival strategies try to share the same space.

THE MISSION:

As you read these stories, look for the Relational Glitch:

The Power Shift: Who is leaning in, and who is pulling back?

The Feedback Loop: How does one person's "safety" move become the other person's "trigger"?

The Unspoken Contract: What are they both trying to protect?

Don't just watch the characters. Watch the space between them.

Chapter 5:

SIGNAL LOSS

He wasn't always distant. That's the part everyone forgets when they tell you to move on. In the beginning, he was everything—a full-strength signal that never wavered.

I remember the first night we stayed up until four a.m. talking. The room was dark, lit only by the soft, rhythmic glow of my laptop charger and the silent blue light of my phone. Every time it buzzed, the sound was sharp and exciting, a frantic little heartbeat on the nightstand. His texts came fast and late, filled with inside jokes that felt like a private language we were inventing in real-time. He used to look at me like I was something rare, his eyes tracing the line of my jaw as if he were trying to memorize a map of a place he never wanted to leave. Back then, the space between us didn't feel like a gap; it felt like a bridge.

So when the signal started to drop, I didn't think it was the end. I thought it was a technical glitch. I thought if I just stood in the right spot, or said the right things, the bars would go back up.

At first, it was little things. The "three dots" of his typing would appear and then vanish into nothing, leaving me staring at a blank gray bubble that felt like a closed door. Plans became "maybe" instead of "definitely." I'd spend hours in my room, the silence of the walls pressing in on me, waiting for a vibration that didn't come. I became a ghost-hunter in our own message thread, scrolling back to the months where the bubbles were constant, trying to find the exact timestamp where the frequency changed. Was it that Tuesday? Did I say too much? Was my heart showing too clearly through the screen?

Three weeks into the "flickering" stage, we met at a diner at midnight. The air inside smelled like burnt coffee and floor wax. We sat in a vinyl booth that was cracked and cold, the fluorescent lights overhead humming with a low, electric anxiety.

I watched him across the table. He was looking at the menu like it held the secrets of the universe, anything to avoid looking at me. I felt the familiar "*Anxious Lean*"—that physical urge to reach across the table and pull his attention back to me.

"You've been quiet lately," I said. I tried to make it sound casual, like I was asking about the weather, but my voice had a jagged edge I couldn't smooth out.

He finally looked up, his eyes weary. "Work's been a lot. I've just needed some space to decompress."

Space. That was the word that always made the floor tilt. To him, space was a lungful of air; to me, it was a lack of oxygen.

I reached for his hand, my fingers brushing the sleeve of his musky cologne-scented hoodie. He didn't pull away, but he didn't squeeze back either. His hand was just... there. A physical presence with no emotional weight.

"I just missed you," I whispered.

He offered a small, sad smile that didn't reach his eyes. "I'm right here."

But he wasn't. Not really. He was in "Airplane Mode," and I was the one frantically trying to find a signal in a dead zone.

We left the diner and stood in the parking lot. The asphalt was damp, reflecting the neon pink of the diner sign in long, distorted streaks. The air was cold, smelling of wet pavement and ozone. He pulled me into a hug, and for a second, the signal was back at full strength. I tucked my face into his neck, breathing him in, telling myself that this—this moment of proximity—was the truth, and the weeks of silence were the lie.

"I'll text you later," he said as he backed away.

I watched his taillights disappear, two red pinpricks in the dark. I waited for that text until the sun came up, my phone clutched in my hand like a lifeline, but the screen stayed dark.

This became our rhythm. A "High" of connection followed by a "Crash" of withdrawal. We'd spend a Saturday together, lost in a movie or a long walk through the park where the trees were just beginning to turn a bruised, autumnal orange. He'd be present, laughing, kissing the top of my head, making me feel like the most important person in the world. And then, as if he'd reached an invisible limit of intimacy, he would vanish.

Until the party.

The basement was crowded, the air thick with the smell of cheap perfume and spilled soda. The music was a physical weight, a bassline that thudded against my ribs like a second, frantic heartbeat. I saw him across the room, leaning against a wood-paneled wall. He was laughing with another girl.

It wasn't that they were doing anything wrong. He wasn't even touching her. But I saw the way he was looking at her—with that hyper-focused, "Full Signal" attention. It was the look he had used on me in the beginning, before the "us" became a weight he had to carry. He looked light. He looked available.

My chest felt like it was being squeezed by an invisible hand. I stood by the snack table, pretending to look at my phone, but the screen was just a blur of meaningless notifications. I felt the "Anxious" panic rising, a hot, prickly heat behind my eyes. I wanted to scream, or run, or pull him away, but I just stood there, drowning in the music.

When I finally confronted him outside, the air was sharp and cold. We stood near a row of overgrown hedges, the leaves rustling like dry paper.

"We're not together," he said, his breath hitching in the chilly air. He looked frustrated, like he was explaining a simple math problem to someone who refused to learn. "I told you I wasn't ready for anything serious. I told you I needed to take things slow."

"I know," I said, my voice shaking so hard it was difficult to form the words. "But you also told me you didn't want to lose me. You can't have it both ways. You can't keep me on a leash just so you don't feel lonely, while I'm over here starving for more than 'maybe'."

He looked at me with a genuine, baffling lack of understanding. To him, keeping me "around" was a kindness. To me, it was a slow-motion heartbreak.

"I don't want to lose you," he repeated, but the words felt hollow now, like a script he'd memorized. "I just don't want to be tied down."

Something finally snapped—a quiet, internal click. It wasn't a blow-up. It was a shutdown. I was tired. I was so tired of standing in the cold parking lots of my own life, waiting for a signal that was never coming back to full strength. I realized then that he wasn't "taking it slow"—he was holding me back.

"So where does that leave me?" I asked.

He didn't answer. He just watched a car drive past, its headlights sweeping over us for a fleeting second before plunging us back into the dark. That was my answer.

"I guess..." he said slowly, "we can keep doing what we're doing."

I nodded, but for the first time, the hope in my chest felt heavier than the heartbreak. I realized that by staying, I was agreeing to a contract where I gave everything and he gave whatever was left over.

A week later, I was back in my room. The afternoon sun was a bruised peach color, casting long shadows of the tree branches against my wall. My phone buzzed.

"You up? Thinking about that diner."

I sat on my bed and watched the phone light up. I thought about the burnt coffee and the cold vinyl. I thought about the "Space" that felt like a canyon. For the first time, I didn't feel the urge to lean forward. I felt the urge to let go.

I let the phone go dark. Then I let it stay dark.

When I finally typed back, my hands were steady.

I can't keep doing this. I need a signal that doesn't drop the second things get real.

He showed up at my door an hour later. The hallway light was casting a yellow shadow behind him. He looked disheveled, his eyes wide with the fear of actually losing the "safety" I provided him.

"I don't want to lose you," he said again, his voice cracking.

"I know," I said. "But I can't keep waiting for you to want more. I've spent months trying to solve you like a puzzle, but the truth is, you're just a door that only opens halfway."

He looked like he wanted to argue, but the truth was finally standing between us, too big to ignore. He wanted the comfort of me without the responsibility of us. He wanted the signal, but he didn't want the commitment of the plan.

I let him go. Not because I stopped caring, but because I realized I was the only one holding the line. I walked back into my apartment and closed the door. The quiet was still there, but for the first time, it didn't feel like a vacuum. It felt like a fresh start.

I checked my phone one last time. No message. And for once, I was perfectly okay with the silence of no signal.

FIRST IMPRESSION CHECK

No analyzing yet. Just what you felt.

When the story ended, I felt:

☐ sad for her

☐ frustrated with him

☐ frustrated with both of them

☐ proud of her for leaving

☐ like this felt familiar

☐ low-key angry

☐ not sure yet

What moment hit you the hardest?

READ BETWEEN THE LINES

This story wasn't about one bad moment.

It was about a pattern.

Which of these showed up?

☐ things were amazing at first

☐ mixed signals started slowly

☐ one person kept hoping it would go back to how it was

☐ the other avoided committing but didn't want to let go

☐ nobody felt fully secure

Anything else you noticed?

WHAT WOULD YOU HAVE DONE?

Be honest. This dynamic is hard.

If you were in her place, would you have:

☐ stayed and kept trying

☐ asked for clearer answers sooner

☐ walked away earlier

☐ accepted the situation as it was

☐ done exactly what she did

Which choice feels most like you?

TIME TO GUESS (JUST FOR FUN)

What attachment styles do you think were interacting here?

☐ Anxious + Secure

☐ Avoidant + Avoidant

☐ Anxious + Avoidant

☐ Fearful-Avoidant + Secure

☐ I'm not sure, but it felt intense

Hold that thought...

THE REVEAL

This story shows an Anxious + Avoidant pairing.

This often looks like:

- one person wanting more closeness
- the other needing more space
- one chasing, the other pulling back
- both feeling misunderstood

Neither person is trying to hurt the other.

They're just responding to closeness in very different ways.

WHY THIS COMBO FEELS SO ADDICTIVE

When someone pulls away, the brain often reacts with:

- increased focus
- stronger emotional attachment
- more urgency to "fix" things

So the more distant someone becomes,

the more intense the connection can feel.

Not because love is growing

but because the nervous system is on high alert.

Relief starts to feel like romance.

Intensity starts to feel like intimacy.

WHY IT HURTS SO MUCH

Because:

- one person feels like they're always reaching
- the other feels like they're always being asked for more
- neither feels fully safe
- both start blaming themselves

And the longer it goes on,

the harder it is to leave — even when you're unhappy.

QUICK SELF-REFLECT

In relationships, I usually:

☐ want more closeness than the other person

☐ want more space than the other person

☐ feel stuck between wanting both

☐ feel calm and steady

☐ not sure yet

When someone pulls away, I usually:

☐ chase

☐ shut down

☐ pretend I don't care

☐ blame myself

☐ leave first

What do I think I was hoping for in those moments?

LAST THOUGHT BEFORE THE NEXT CHAPTER

Wanting someone who can't meet you where you are doesn't mean you're unlovable.

It usually means your needs and their fears are colliding.

Next, we'll look at what happens when both people want closeness —

but in very different ways.

Chapter 6:

FULL SIGNAL, NO CONNECTION

I knew something was wrong the moment she didn't text me back. Not because she usually texted fast — she didn't — but because my brain had already decided today was the day things changed. She had said she'd call after practice, and when she didn't, I watched the clock like it was counting down to something bad. Every minute that passed felt heavier. Maybe she forgot. Maybe she was busy. Maybe she didn't want to talk to me anymore. Maybe she was already pulling away and I just hadn't caught up yet.

By the time my phone finally buzzed, my stomach was already tight.

Sorry, got held late. On my way home now.

That was it. No heart. No extra explanation. No *I missed you.* Just... normal.

I should've felt better. I didn't.

When she finally called, I answered on the first ring. "Are you okay?" I asked.

She laughed softly. "Yeah. Why wouldn't I be?"

I didn't know how to explain that I had already lived three different breakups in my head while I was waiting. "I don't know," I said. "You just seemed kind of off earlier."

"I was just tired," she said. "Nothing's wrong."

She said it like it was obvious. Like I was worrying over nothing. Which made me feel stupid for asking, but also not convinced.

"So... you're not mad at me or anything?" I asked.

She went quiet for a second. "No," she said. "Why would I be?"

I didn't have a good answer for that, because nothing had actually happened. "I just wanted to make sure," I said.

"You don't have to keep checking," she said gently. "If something's wrong, I'll tell you."

That should've been comforting. Instead, it felt like she didn't understand how loud my head gets when things go quiet.

We talked about our days. Homework. Her coach. My brother being annoying. Everything sounded fine, which somehow made me feel worse. Because if everything was fine, then why did I feel like I was always one wrong move away from losing her?

A few days later, she told me she was going out with friends. "Cool," I said. "Have fun." I meant it. Mostly.

Later, I saw pictures of her laughing with people I didn't know. Something twisted in my chest. She looked happy. Not missing me. Not checking her phone. Not worried. Just... okay.

When I texted her, she didn't answer right away. So I waited. And waited. And told myself not to spiral. I failed at that. By the time she replied, I'd already convinced myself she was drifting.

"You good?" I asked.

"Yeah," she said. "Just busy."

Busy. I hated that word. Not because it was wrong — but because it meant I wasn't the center of her world the way she was becoming the center of mine.

The next day, I tried to act normal. I told myself I wouldn't overthink things. I wouldn't look for signs. I wouldn't ask for reassurance.

I made it about three hours.

She took longer than usual to answer a message. Not that long — just long enough for me to notice.

I stared at the conversation, rereading my last text like it might explain something.

Did I say something wrong?

When she finally replied, it was casual. Like nothing had happened.

Which, technically, nothing had.

Still, I asked, "Everything okay?"

"Yeah," she said. "Just helping my mom with something."

"Oh," I said. "Okay."

I hated how relieved I felt.

Later that week, we were sitting together, and she was telling me about something funny that happened in class. I was listening, but part of me was still scanning for distance, for signs, for anything that might tell me how secure I should feel.

"You seem quiet," she said.

"I'm just tired," I said.

She nodded, accepting that answer easily.

I wondered what it would feel like to believe something that simply.

A week later, I finally said it out loud.

"I feel like I care more than you do," I told her.

She looked surprised. "That's not true."

"Then why does it always feel like I'm the one worried about losing you?"

She took a breath. "Because I'm not worried about losing you."

That should've been reassuring. Instead, it made my chest ache.

"How can you not be?" I asked.

"Because we're good," she said. "And if we're not, we'll talk about it."

I stared at her, not sure how to explain that calm felt like distance when you're used to bracing for impact.

"I just wish you reacted more," I said.

"To what?" she asked. "Nothing is happening."

I didn't know how to tell her that something was always happening inside me.

"I don't want to be the only one who feels this," I said.

She reached for my hand. "You're not alone in this," she said quietly. "I just don't live in worst-case scenarios."

I wanted to borrow that part of her. Instead, I felt like something was wrong with me.

We didn't break up that night. Nothing dramatic happened. But I started feeling like I was asking for something she didn't know how to give, and she started feeling like she was being blamed for not being afraid enough.

The conversations became softer after that, but also more careful. I stopped asking some questions. She stopped trying to reassure me as much. Not because she didn't care, but because she thought everything was okay.

I kept waiting for the moment when I would finally feel settled.

It didn't come.

A few weeks later, I ended it. Not because she did anything wrong, but because I was tired of feeling like I loved her louder.

She cried. I did too.

She told me she would've stayed.

I told her I couldn't keep wondering if I mattered.

And the worst part is, I think we were both telling the truth.

FIRST IMPRESSION CHECK

No right answers. Just what you felt.

When the story ended, I felt:

☐ sad for both of them

☐ frustrated with him

☐ frustrated with her

☐ like nobody was really wrong

☐ like I recognized myself

☐ confused about who I agreed with

☐ not sure yet

What part of the story stayed with you most?

READ BETWEEN THE LINES

This story wasn't about cheating or fighting.

It was about how two people experience safety differently.

Which of these showed up?

☐ one person needing lots of reassurance

☐ the other trusting things were fine

☐ calm being mistaken for distance

☐ worry being mistaken for pressure

☐ both people feeling misunderstood

Anything else you noticed?

WHAT WOULD YOU HAVE DONE?

This one's tricky.

If you were in his place, would you have:

☐ asked for more reassurance

☐ tried to worry less

☐ stayed and worked through it

☐ taken space like he did

☐ not sure what I'd do

If you were in her place, would you have:

☐ reassured him more

☐ felt overwhelmed

☐ wondered what you were doing wrong

☐ stayed calm anyway

☐ felt blamed for not reacting enough

Which side felt more like you?

TIME TO GUESS (JUST FOR FUN)

What attachment styles do you think were interacting here?

☐ Secure + Secure

☐ Secure + Anxious

☐ Anxious + Anxious

☐ Avoidant + Anxious

☐ Not sure, but it felt unbalanced

Hold that thought...

THE REVEAL

This story shows a Secure + Anxious pairing.

This can look like:

- one person trusting the relationship
- the other constantly scanning for danger
- one feeling pressured
- the other feeling alone

No one is wrong.

They just feel safe in different ways.

REAL TALK MOMENT

Secure people don’t panic when things go quiet.

Anxious people don’t relax just because nothing is wrong.

Both are trying to protect the relationship.

They’re just using different strategies.

And sometimes, even when there’s real care,

those strategies don’t line up.

QUICK SELF-REFLECT

When someone doesn't worry as much as I do, I usually feel:

☐ relieved

☐ confused

☐ more anxious

☐ unimportant

☐ calmer after a while

When someone worries more than I do, I usually feel:

☐ protective

☐ pressured

☐ responsible for their feelings

☐ patient

☐ unsure how to help

What do I think I was hoping for in that relationship?

LAST THOUGHT BEFORE THE NEXT CHAPTER

Sometimes love isn't about how much you care.

It's about whether you feel safe caring the way you do.

Chapter 7:

UNREAD

He texts me before I even get home. The screen of my phone lights up in the cup holder of my car, a small, white intrusion in the dark.

Did you make it?

I stare at it while the engine idles. We were together ten minutes ago. I can still feel the ghost of his hand on my shoulder, a weight that felt less like affection and more like an anchor.

Yeah, I type back. *I'm good*.

Three dots appear immediately. My chest tightens. The dots are a demand—a silent expectation for always wanting more.

You seemed off when you left.

I exhale slowly, the sound loud in the cramped car.

"I wasn't off," I mutter to the empty seats.

Just tired, I send.

Pause.

The air in the car feels thin. I know what's coming. I can feel the invisible thread he's trying to tie to me, pulling, asking for a reassurance I don't know how to manufacture on command.

Then:

Did I do something?

There it is. That shift. That sudden, heavy requirement to manage someone else's emotions.

"No," I say out loud, sharper than I mean to.

I don't answer right away this time. I walk into my apartment, the silence of the rooms a relief. I change into sweats, trying to shake the feeling of being watched, even though I'm alone. But by the time I pick the phone back up, the thread has tightened.

I just don't want things to feel weird between us.

They don't feel weird. They feel... monitored. Like every flicker of my expression is a riddle he's obsessed with solving.

Nothing's weird, I reply, my thumbs feeling heavy. *You're overthinking.*

I toss my phone onto the bed like that settles it. Like I've successfully pushed the world back an inch. It doesn't settle anything. It just starts the clock.

The next day, he's normal again. Smiling. Easy. That's what confuses me. How he can go from the edge of a cliff to perfectly fine so quickly. We sit together at lunch, his knee pressed against mine under the table. It's a nice heat, but I find myself shifting my leg just enough to break the contact.

"You're okay today?" he asks, his eyes scanning mine.

I laugh, but it feels hollow. "I was okay yesterday."

"I know, I just—" He stops himself, looking down at his food. "Never mind."

No. Not never mind. I can feel the question sitting there between us, a third person at the table.

"What?" I ask.

He hesitates. "I just feel like sometimes you pull away, and I don't know why. It makes me feel like I'm losing you while I'm looking at you."

My chest reaches that familiar limit. The walls move in.

"I don't pull away," I say, my voice flat.

He gives me a look. Not accusing. Just... sure. "You do," he says gently. "And I just want to understand the map. I want to know where the 'no-go' zones are."

Understand it. Like I'm a puzzle. Like if he just finds the right piece, he'll own the whole picture.

"There's nothing to understand," I say. "I just don't think everything needs to be a post-mortem conversation."

"I'm not trying to analyze you," he says. "I just care about you."

And there it is. That word. Care. It should feel like a safety net. Instead, it feels like a cage. It feels like a debt I didn't sign for, with interest I can't afford to pay.

Later that night, we're on FaceTime. The glow of the screen makes his eyes look wider, more searching. He's quieter this time, just watching me.

"What?" I say finally, the irritation bubbling up.

"Nothing."

"Then stop looking at me like that."

"Like what?"

"Like I'm about to evaporate. Like I'm a ghost."

He exhales, a ragged sound over the speaker. "That's kind of what it feels like sometimes. Like you're physically there, but you've already left the room mentally."

Something in me snaps. The pressure—the constant, relentless reaching—becomes too much.

"I'm literally right here," I say. "What more do you want? Do you want my blood? My every thought?"

"I don't know," he says, his voice breaking. "Maybe just... reassurance? That you actually want to be in this? That you aren't just waiting for the exit sign?"

My stomach drops. There it is. The question underneath all the other questions. I could answer it. I could say yes, I want this. I could reach through the screen and make it easier. Instead,

I feel the familiar coldness wash over me. It's my armor. It's how I survive.

"Why do I have to keep proving my existence to you?" I ask.

"I'm not asking you to prove it," he says. "I'm just asking you to say it."

"It's the same thing," I shoot back. "Because the second I say it, there's a new set of expectations. A new level of pressure. I say it once, and then you'll need to hear it ten more times tomorrow just to believe me."

"I just want to feel like I matter," he whispers.

"You do," I say quickly. Too quickly.

"Then why does it feel like I'm the only one fighting for this?"

The words hit harder than I expect because they're not entirely wrong. But not for the reason he thinks. I care. I just don't know how to act like it without feeling like I'm giving up pieces of myself until there's nothing left.

"I think you just need more than I have," I say.

The silence that follows is absolute.

Then, quieter: "That doesn't mean I'm wrong for needing it."

I rub my forehead, suddenly exhausted down to my marrow.

“I didn’t say you were wrong,” I say. “I just can’t be the person who fills that hole for you.”

The second the words leave my mouth, I feel the shift. The irreversible drop.

“So that’s it?” he asks.

I shrug. “I just don’t think this works. It’s too loud. All of it.”

He looks at me like he’s seeing a stranger. “Because I asked you how you feel?”

“Because the asking feels like a demand,” I say.

We don’t talk after that. No long goodbye. Just a quiet stop.

And for a few days, I feel lighter. I wake up and my phone is silent. No questions. No "off" moods to explain. No weight on my chest. I have my rooms back. I have my head back.

Then, a week later, I open our old messages.

Just for a second.

And I see his last text—the one I never replied to. And I feel it. That small, sharp ache in the center of my chest. It’s not enough to make me call him. It’s not enough to change the ending. But it’s enough to notice. He wasn’t too much. He was just holding up a mirror, and I didn’t like the person I saw when I was with him. I wasn't as unbothered as I pretended to be. I was just better at hiding how much I was shaking.

FIRST IMPRESSION CHECK

No right answers. Just what you felt.

When the story ended, I felt:

☐ A sense of relief for her

☐ Heartbreak for him

☐ Frustration at the lack of communication

☐ Like I've said those exact words before

☐ Like I've heard those exact words before

What was the "heaviest" moment in the story for you?

READ BETWEEN THE LINES

This story wasn't about being "mean" or "needy."

It was about how two people experience safety differently.

Which of these showed up?

☐ one person's "care" feeling like "pressure"

☐ "I'm right here" being mistaken for "I'm all in"

☐ silence being used as a shield

☐ worry being mistaken for an accusation

☐ both people feeling misunderstood

Anything else you noticed?

WHAT WOULD YOU HAVE DONE?

This one's tricky.

If you were in her place, would you have:

☐ explained why you felt pressured

☐ tried to give the reassurance he asked for

☐ stayed and worked through it

☐ taken space like she did

☐ not sure what I'd do

If you were in his place, would you have:

☐ stopped asking questions

☐ felt overwhelmed

☐ wondered what you were doing wrong

☐ stayed calm anyway

☐ walked away sooner

Which side felt more like you?

TIME TO GUESS (JUST FOR FUN)

What attachment styles do you think were interacting here?

☐ Secure + Secure

☐ Secure + Anxious

☐ Anxious + Anxious

☐ Avoidant + Anxious

☐ Not sure, but it felt unbalanced

Hold that thought...

THE REVEAL

This is the Anxious-Avoidant Trap.

It is a dance where neither person is "wrong," but their steps don't match.

The Anxious Partner interprets silence as a threat. They move closer to find safety.

The Avoidant Partner interprets closeness as a threat. They move away to find safety.

The tragedy of this dynamic is that the more the Anxious partner tries to "save" the relationship, the more the Avoidant partner feels they need to "save" themselves from it.

REAL TALK MOMENT

Avoidant people don't pull away because they don't care.

They pull away because they are afraid of losing themselves.

Anxious people don't ask questions to be annoying.

They ask because they are afraid of losing the connection.

And sometimes, even when there's real care,

those strategies collide rather than connect.

QUICK SELF-REFLECT

When someone wants more from me than I can give, I usually feel:

☐ guilty

☐ pressured

☐ responsible for them

☐ like I want to run

When someone pulls away from me, I usually feel:

☐ panicked

☐ unimportant

☐ like I need to fix it

☐ rejected

LAST THOUGHT BEFORE THE NEXT CHAPTER

Sometimes love isn't about how much you care.

It's about whether you feel safe caring the way you do.

Chapter 8:

DELIVERED

The blue light of the smartphone was the only thing illuminating the apartment, a cold, clinical glow that made the shadows in the corners of the living room look deeper than they were. The text had been sitting there for three hours, three minutes, and twelve seconds.

Brunch Sunday? My treat!

To anyone else, it was a warm gesture. To me, it looked like a summons. It looked like a bill coming due.

I stared at the screen until the words blurred into illegible black smudges. My thumb hovered over the glass, trembling slightly. I wanted to throw the phone across the room. I wanted to submerge it in a bowl of water until the light died. Instead, I just watched the clock on the corner of the screen tick forward.

Twenty-four hours ago, I had committed the ultimate act of treason against myself. Sarah and I had been on the phone for four hours—a marathon of exposure that had left me feeling like I had been peeled like a fruit. I had told her about the way my chest feels like it's being seized in a tightening fist whenever my boss raises his voice. I'd told her about the recurring dream where I'm screaming in a crowded room and no one even turns their head. She had listened with a quiet, steady patience that was more terrifying than any judgment could have been. She hadn't interrupted. She hadn't tried to fix me or offer advice. She had just... been there.

And that was the problem. Now, she was "there." She was inside the perimeter. She had seen the messy, uncurated basement of my psyche, and now I felt like I was walking around without my skin.

I stood up and paced the length of my kitchen, the linoleum cold against my bare feet. I need to move, I thought, and I wasn't thinking about the next room. I was thinking about Montana. Or Maine. Somewhere where the air was too cold for people to stand close to each other. I could change my name. I could start over as someone who never spoke for more than five minutes at a time. I could be a ghost in a small town, a person with no history and no "marathons" to regret.

My heart was doing that hollow, frantic thud—the sound of a fist hitting a locked door from the inside. I felt raw. It was the same feeling as leaving your front door wide open in a bad neighborhood and going to sleep. Any minute now, she was going to walk in and start rearranging the furniture of my life. She would decide my favorite mug was ugly. She would tell me my coping mechanisms were dull. She would see the flaw, the big, jagged one I try to hide with humor and work ethic and then the look in her eyes would change.

I knew that look. It starts as sympathy and ends as a quiet, polite exit.

I sat back down, my breath coming in shallow hitches. I couldn't do Sunday. Sunday meant eye contact. Sunday meant she might ask a follow-up question about the dream. She might ask one simple, honest question, and the hairline fractures in my composure would finally split wide open.

I'm busy Sunday, I typed, my fingers moving with a mechanical coldness. *Maybe next time.*

I turned the phone face down on the coffee table. The silence of the apartment rushed back in, heavy and suffocating, but safe. I had successfully reinforced the barricade.

Monday morning felt like a funeral procession. The office was a sea of beige carpets and the buzzing of fluorescent lights that always seemed to vibrate at a frequency meant to induce headaches. I stayed in my cubicle, my eyes glued to spreadsheets, creating a fortress of productivity. If I looked busy enough, I was invisible. I wore my "work face," the one that was pleasant but distant, the one that never invited personal questions.

But then came the 10:30 coffee break. My body needed the caffeine, but my brain warned me of the "neutral zone." The breakroom was where the professional mask usually slipped, where people talked about their weekends and their kids and their lives.

I saw her as soon as I rounded the corner. Sarah was standing by the Keurig, her back to me. She was wearing a bright yellow sweater, the kind of color people wear when they aren't afraid of being noticed. It was a loud, happy color that felt like a physical blow to my chest.

I considered turning around, retreating to the safety of my cubicle and drinking lukewarm water instead, but she sensed me. She turned, and her face lit up with a genuine, effortless warmth.

"Hey!" she said. The sound of her voice felt like a hand reaching out to grab mine, and I instinctively pulled back, even though she hadn't moved. "Missed you yesterday. You okay? You sounded a little stressed in your text."

She stepped closer, entering my personal bubble. The air in the breakroom suddenly felt very thin, like we were standing on a mountain peak where the oxygen had been sucked away.

"I'm fine," I said. My voice sounded like it belonged to a stranger, clipped, professional, and freezing. "Just a lot going on. Projects. Life."

"I get it," she said softly. She reached out, her hand moving toward my arm in a casual, friendly gesture of comfort.

I flinched.

It wasn't a big movement, just a sharp, involuntary jerk of my shoulder, but it might as well have been a scream. Sarah's hand froze in mid-air. Her fingers curled back into her palm, and she dropped her arm to her side.

The light in her eyes didn't go out, but it dimmed. A flicker of confusion crossed her face, followed by something worse: pity. Or maybe it was just the realization that she was standing too close to someone who didn't want to be touched.

"I'm sorry," she said, her voice dropping an octave. "I didn't mean to startle you. I just... well, if you need to talk about anything from the other night, or if things are just feeling heavy—"

"I don't," I snapped.

The words were out before I could filter them. They hung in the air like a physical boundary, a 'no trespassing' sign hammered into the floor between our shoes. I saw her recoil slightly, her posture stiffening.

Apologize, the small, rational part of my brain whispered. Tell her you're just overwhelmed. Tell her that her kindness feels like a spotlight you're not ready to stand under. Tell her she's the only person you actually trust.

Instead, the louder part of my brain—the part that lives in the bunker took over. It looked at her hurt expression and interpreted it as a countdown. She's going to get tired of this, the voice hissed. She's going to realize you're too much work. She's going to realize that being your friend is like trying to hug a cactus. She's going to leave anyway, so you might as well finish it now. End it on your terms. Don't let her be the one to walk away first.

"I actually have a meeting I'm late for," I lied, my eyes fixed on a point somewhere over her left shoulder.

I stepped past her, the scent of her perfume—something light and floral, feeling like an accusation. I didn't look back. I didn't want to see the moment her smile finally, completely disappeared.

I didn't text her for the rest of the week.

Each day was a grueling exercise in self-restraint. I would pick up my phone, open our message thread, and stare at the "Maybe next time" I had sent. I wanted to tell her about a funny dog I saw, or a weird email from accounting. I wanted to tell her that I missed our four-hour talks, even if they terrified me.

But every time I started to type, the panic would flare up. If I texted her, I was inviting her back in. I was giving her permission to care about me. I was giving her the power to hurt me again.

I told myself I was "giving her space." I told myself I was being the bigger person by not "burdening" her with my moods. I convinced myself that she was probably relieved to have a break from me.

But really, I was waiting.

I was waiting for the inevitable moment she stopped trying. I was waiting for the silence to become permanent, so I could finally say, See? Everyone leaves. I was right to be careful. It was a self-fulfilling prophecy I was nurturing like a sick pet, feeding it with my own isolation.

By Friday evening, the silence was deafening. I was sitting on my sofa, the TV muted, watching the rain streak against the glass. I felt like I was underwater, the pressure of the unspoken words pressing against my ribs.

Then, the phone vibrated.

The caller: Sarah.

I didn't pick up. I sat there and watched the phone dance across the coffee table, the dancing vibration echoing through the empty room. It rang and rang, a desperate little heartbeat on the mahogany surface.

Pick it up, one side of me screamed. She's your person. She's the only one who stayed after seeing the basement. Pick it up and say you're sorry. Tell her you're scared. Just say the words.

Don't let her in, the other part whispered, cold and venomous. She's only calling because she feels guilty. Or she's calling to tell you she's done. If you don't pick up, she can't reject you. You can't be abandoned if you're already gone. Stay in the bunker. It's dark, but nothing hits you here.

The ringing stopped. The silence that followed was even worse, it was hollow.

Ten minutes later, the text arrived.

I don't know what happened, but I feel like I'm walking on eggshells. Did I upset you? I really value our friendship, but I don't know how to reach you right now.

I felt a surge of heat. It wasn't sadness—it was a defensive, white-hot spark. My brain seized on the word "eggshells." It felt like an attack on my character.

Oh, so now I'm the problem? I thought. Now I'm the one making things difficult?

It was a pivot. A survival tactic. If I could make her the "dramatic" one, then I wasn't the "broken" one. If I could turn her concern into an attack, I had a reason to fight back. I had a reason to push her away that felt like self-defense instead of self-destruction.

My thumb flew over the keyboard.

You're being dramatic, I sent. *I've just been busy at work. It's just a calendar, Sarah. Not everything is a deep-seated emotional mystery for you to solve. I can't be on call 24/7 just because you're feeling insecure about a missed brunch.*

I watched the "Read" receipt appear instantly. My heart was thumping so hard I could hear it in my ears.

I waited. I actually felt a sick sense of anticipation. I wanted her to yell. I wanted her to call me heartless, or cold, or a bad friend. If she yelled, I could justify my exit. I could say, I don't need this drama in my life, and walk away with my head held high, convinced that I was the victim of her "neediness."

But Sarah didn't fight.

The three dots appeared, disappeared, then appeared again.

I'm sorry you feel that way, she finally replied. I didn't realize I was being a burden. I'll back off. Take care.

The "Take care" felt like a door locking from the outside. Not a slamming door, but a quiet, final click.

I stared at the screen. The "Read" receipt was gone. The conversation was over. The marathon was finished.

I put the phone down. I walked to the window and looked out at the streetlights reflecting in the puddles. The walls were back up. The perimeter was secure. No one was looking at me. No one was touching my arm. No one knew about my dreams or my boss or the way my chest tightened.

I was perfectly, entirely safe.

And as I stood there in the quiet of my reinforced fortress, I realized I had never felt more alone in my entire life. I had won the war against being known, and my prize was an empty room.

Tuesday was the hardest. Tuesday is when the silence stops feeling like a choice and starts feeling like a haunting.

I sat at my desk, the dual monitors cast a steady glow across my keyboard, my inbox filling with low-stakes emergencies from people who didn't know my middle name. I liked them for that. I liked the mailroom guy who only knew me as "Suite 402." I liked the IT guy who thought I was just a person who forgot their password once a month. To them, I was a finished product. I was a statue. No cracks, no basement, no screaming dreams.

But knowing Sarah was three rows down felt like a hairline crack in my foundation—small, quiet, and capable of bringing the whole house down.

She's probably talking about you, the Voice whispered. The Voice didn't have a name, but it had been with me since I was six, sitting on a suitcase in a hallway, waiting for a car that never came. She's in the breakroom right now, telling Mark from Accounting how 'heavy' you were on the phone. She's laughing about the tightness in your chest. She's dissecting your 'marathon of exposure' like a biology project.

I gripped my mouse so hard my knuckles turned white. She wouldn't do that, I argued back. Sarah isn't like that. She was kind. She listened.

That's the trap, the Voice countered, smooth and cold. Kindness is just a down payment on future leverage. She's building a file on you. Every secret you gave her is a weapon she can use when she gets bored. And she will get bored. Look at you. You're exhausting. Even you don't want to be in your head—why would she?

I opened a spreadsheet. I deleted a row of data. I added it back.

The internal monologue wasn't a conversation; it was a courtroom. I was the defendant, the prosecutor, and the biased judge. The evidence against me was my own history: the friends who drifted away when I got "too real," the partners who called me "mysterious" until they realized "mysterious" just meant "emotionally unavailable."

She saw me, I thought, and a cold shiver traced my spine. She saw the part of me that doesn't know how to be a person.

By Wednesday, the monologue had shifted from fear to a strange, twisted form of arrogance.

I'm doing her a favor, I told myself as I walked past her empty desk. She thinks she wants to help, but she's out of her depth. I'm the hero here. I'm the one pulling the plug before she gets electrocuted by my dysfunction. I'm saving her from the inevitable disappointment of knowing the real me.

This was the "Selfless Martyr" defense. It was a comfortable lie. It allowed me to feel noble while I was being cruel. It turned my cowardice into a sacrifice.

I imagined Sarah at her desk, typing away, her yellow sweater a distant beacon. I wondered if she was looking at her phone, waiting for a text. I wondered if she felt the "eggshells." I hoped she did. Not because I wanted her to hurt, but because if she was uncomfortable, she would leave. And if she left, the tension would finally break.

Just leave, I pleaded silently, staring at the back of her head from across the floor. Stop being so consistent. Stop being so 'there.' Be the person the Voice says you are, so I can finally breathe again.

Thursday was the "Ghosting" phase. I started to delete our history. Not the digital one—not yet—but the mental one. I replayed our four-hour call, but I edited it. I made my own voice sound pathetic. I made her silence sound like judgment. I convinced myself that when she said, "I'm here for you," she was actually saying, "I'm obligated to pity you."

You're a project to her, the Voice decided. She's a 'fixer.' She doesn't like you; she likes the feeling of being the one who saved you. And once you're 'fixed,' she'll find a new broken toy.

This was the most effective shield of all: the "Mercenary Motive." If I could convince myself Sarah's kindness was selfish, I didn't owe her anything. I didn't owe her brunch. I didn't owe her an explanation. I certainly didn't owe her my heart.

But then, Friday afternoon arrived. The office began to empty. The weekend loomed, forty-eight hours of unstructured time where the silence wouldn't be a shield, but a mirror.

I stood by the elevator, my bag slung over my shoulder. The doors opened, and there she was.

She didn't look angry. She didn't look like a "mercenary fixer." She looked tired. There were faint circles under her eyes, and her yellow sweater looked rumpled. She looked at me, and for a second, the boardroom in my head went silent.

"Have a good weekend," she said. It wasn't a question. It wasn't an invite. It was a grace note.

I should have said, You too. I should have said, I'm sorry I've been a ghost.

"Yeah," I muttered, stepping into the elevator as she stepped out. "You too."

As the doors slid shut, the Voice came back with a vengeance. See? She's fine. She didn't even try to stop you. She's already moving on. She never cared at all.

The elevator descended, and with every floor, the walls in my chest grew a foot taller. By the time I reached the lobby, I was a fortress again. I was "safe." I was unreachable.

And I was absolutely, devastatingly terrified of the quiet apartment waiting for me at home.

FIRST IMPRESSION CHECK

No right answers. Just what you felt.

When the story ended, I felt:

☐ exhausted for both of them

☐ like I finally understood that "push-pull" feeling

☐ sad that the friendship ended over nothing

☐ like I've been the one "flinching" before

☐ like I've been the one "walking on eggshells"

What was the most uncomfortable moment for you?

READ BETWEEN THE LINES

Which of these did you see?

☐ "Vulnerability Hangover" (feeling exposed after sharing)

☐ Flinching at physical or emotional closeness

☐ Waiting for the "inevitable" betrayal

☐ Creating a conflict just to end the tension

☐ Sabotaging a good thing before it can "fail"

WHAT WOULD YOU HAVE DONE?

If you were in her place, would you have:

☐ kept trying to reach her

☐ given her the space she asked for, even if it hurt

☐ told her how her coldness made you feel

☐ walked away sooner to protect yourself

If you were in the narrator's place, would you have:

☐ told her you were feeling overwhelmed by the closeness

☐ apologized for the "snap"

☐ forced yourself to go to brunch anyway

☐ realized your fear was lying to you

Which side felt more like you?

THE REVEAL

This story shows Fearful-Avoidant (Disorganized) attachment. Fearful-Avoidant attachment is the "Disorganized" style. It's a conflict between the need to belong and the need to survive.

Unlike the dismissive-avoidant (who simply values independence), the fearful-avoidant wants closeness but views it as dangerous.

The Trigger: High levels of intimacy or vulnerability.

The Reaction: A sudden shift from "all in" to "get out."

The Result: Relationships that feel like a rollercoaster of intense connection followed by cold withdrawal.

REAL TALK MOMENT

Fearful-avoidant people often grew up in environments where the people who were supposed to provide safety were also the source of fear.

As adults, when someone gets "too close," the brain's alarm system goes off. It's not that they don't love you—it's that their brain is trying to protect them from a hurt it's sure is coming.

LAST THOUGHT BEFORE THE NEXT CHAPTER

The hardest part of loyalty isn't the staying—it's the refusal to retreat when the 'marathon of exposure' makes you want to vanish into a different life.

PART III:

You Are Not One Thing

Integration & Evolution

If Part I was the Incoming Alert and Part II was the Communication Breakdown, Part III is about Recalibrating the Interface.

We often treat our attachment style like a factory setting—a permanent "Do Not Disturb" mode or a "Read Receipt" we can't turn off. But the truth is, your internal software is more fluid than you think. You can be Auto-Reply: Secure at your desk and Network Error: Anxious at a dinner table. This section is about reclaiming the Admin rights to your own heart and realizing that while you built these firewalls to survive a breach, you are allowed to lower the security level when the connection is safe.

THE MISSION:

As you navigate these final chapters, look for the Internal Pivot:

The Situational Signal: Why do you have a "Strong Connection" with a friend but "No Service" in a relationship? What changes when the network shifts?

The Three-Second Buffer: Can you find the space between the "Notification" and the "Snap"? Can you choose a truth over a defensive auto-reply?

The Person Behind the Profile: How do you strip away the clinical "Exposure" to see the human underneath—the one who is just trying to find a signal in a world full of static?

Don't just diagnose the "Glitch." Watch the architecture of who you are becoming.

Chapter 9:

SIGNAL AND STRENGTH

THE FOUR BASE SIGNALS

Before we look at how your signal shifts, we need to define the four primary ways our hearts learned to survive. Every story you've read in this book so far has been a portrait of one of these four "User Interfaces":

1. Secure Attachment: The Strong Connection

This is the "Ideal Signal." You are comfortable with both closeness and independence. You don't view a "Read" receipt as a threat, and you don't feel the need to vanish when a conversation gets deep. You trust that the link is stable, even when the other person is offline.

2. Anxious Attachment: The Search for Service

This is the "Hyper-Vigilant Signal." You crave closeness but are constantly scanning for signs of abandonment. You might double-text to "verify the link" or feel a "System Error" if someone takes too long to reply. For you, silence isn't just quiet—it's a sign of a dropped connection.

3. Avoidant Attachment: The Airplane Mode

This is the "Self-Sufficient Signal." You value independence so much that intimacy can feel like a "Security Breach." When things get too "real," your reflex is to de-activate, put the phone on silent, and pull back into your own bunker. You've learned that the only way to stay safe is to remain unreachable.

4. Fearful Avoidant (Disorganized): The System Crash

This is the "Conflict Signal." It involves wanting to run toward someone and away from them at the exact same time. It feels like a "Glitch" in the hardware—you desperately want the warmth of the connection, but as soon as you get it, your internal alarm goes off, telling you that being seen is dangerous. It is a state of "fright without solution."

WHY YOUR SIGNAL SHIFTS: TERRITORY MATTERS

Attachment is contextual. Contextual means the signal changes depending on the environment. Your "Internal Working Model" isn't one big map; it's a series of different maps you use for different relationships. This is why you can feel like a totally different person depending on whose name pops up on your screen. Here is an example of how you could possibly experience multiple styles with different people.

Secure with Friends: The Safe Network

Many people who are "Anxious" in dating are surprisingly Secure with their friends. Why? Because the "Cost of Connection" feels lower. You aren't worried about a best friend "deleting" you if you don't text back for three hours. You trust the long-term stability of the link, so you stay "Visible" without the panic. You are able to be your most authentic self because the "Firewall" isn't necessary.

Anxious in Dating: The Romantic Hotspot

Dating is the ultimate "High-Bandwidth Zone." Because the stakes feel so high and the biological desire for "Proximity" is so intense, your most primitive attachment signals are triggered here. You might be the most confident, Secure person in your friend group, but the moment you start "Catching Feelings," you revert to a "Network Error" state, checking your phone every thirty seconds to see if the signal has moved.

Avoidant with Family: The Original Blueprint

Family is where your Original Code was written. Even a Secure adult can find themselves "Going Offline" or becoming "Dismissive" the moment they step into their childhood home. You might "Ghost" your parents' calls or give one-word answers to protect your autonomy. In this territory, you are often reacting to the "Legacy Server"—the person you had to be to survive your upbringing.

STRESS: THE PEAK TRAFFIC EVENT

Your attachment style is most visible when the "Network" is under heavy load. Stress, whether it's finals week, a job loss, or a high-stakes argument—causes your system to default to its most defensive "Survival Mode."

But why does this happen? To your brain, stress is a bandwidth thief. Under normal circumstances, you have enough "mental RAM" to run your high-level logic, the part of you that knows your partner is just busy or that your friend isn't ignoring you on purpose. But when external stress spikes, your brain enters a Power-Save Mode. It shuts down the complex, logical apps and reverts to the most basic, hard-coded survival scripts.

In this state, the "threat" is no longer the job loss or the exam; the threat is the loss of the connection that makes you feel safe. Here is how that "System Overload" plays out in real-time:

Anxious Overload: Hyper-activation

Stress leads to a desperate need for Proximity. When your external world feels chaotic, your internal system interprets any silence from a loved one as a "Network Failure."

The Logic: "If I can just get them to reply, I'll know I'm not alone in this storm."

The Glitch: You search for constant reassurance, double-texting or creating "tests" to see if they still care. You might become "clingy" or demanding, but it's actually a frantic attempt to stabilize the signal because you feel like you're drifting out to sea.

Avoidant Overload: De-activation

Stress triggers a total System Shutdown. When the world gets too loud, your brain decides that other people are just "extra noise" you can't afford to process.

The Logic: "I can only survive this if I cut all the power lines and focus on the task at hand."

The Glitch: You minimize your emotions and treat intimacy like a "Battery Drain." You pull back into total, exhausting isolation, putting your feelings in a "Vault" and throwing away the key until the storm passes. You don't just want space; you want to be invisible so nothing else can demand anything from you.

Fearful-Avoidant (Disorganized) Overload: System Crash

High stress leads to an internal paradox. Because your "Safe Haven" was historically also a "Source of Fear," stress creates a feedback loop that the system can't handle.

The Logic: "I'm drowning and I need you to save me, but if you get too close, you'll drown me too."

The Glitch: This is the most painful state—the fright without solution. You might lash out in a hot, defensive spark to push someone away, only to immediately collapse and beg them to stay. The internal conflict becomes a "denial of service" attack on your own heart; the signals cross, the wires smoke, and the system simply stops functioning.

THE ADMIN HACK: COPY-PASTING YOUR SECURITY

The most empowering realization you can have in this chapter is that Secure Attachment is not a foreign language; it's a dialect you already speak. You aren't a broken device that needs a factory rebuild; you are a complex network that simply has a few "dead zones" where the signal keeps dropping.

Healing isn't about installing entirely new hardware from scratch. It's about Internal Open-Sourcing. It's the process of looking at the parts of your life where your "Connection" is already strong and stable, and learning how to Copy-Paste that Secure Code into the relationships where you are currently glitching.

FINDING YOUR "SOURCE CODE"

To start the hack, you have to identify your Safe Network. Think of the person—or even the environment—where you feel the most "Offline" from your defenses.

Is it with a best friend who has seen you at your absolute worst and didn't hit "Delete"?

Is it with a pet who offers a "Constant Signal" of affection without any subtext?

Is it in a hobby or a workspace where you feel "Competent" and "Secure" in your abilities?

In these spaces, you aren't checking the "Read" receipts of your worth every thirty seconds. You aren't "De-activating" or "Hyper-activating." You are just... existing. This is your Secure Baseline. This is the evidence that the software is already installed on your hard drive.

HOW TO RUN THE "COPY-PASTE" COMMAND

Once you identify what "Secure" feels like in your body, you can begin the manual override in your high-stakes relationships. It's a three-step process:

Analyze the Metadata: When you are with your "Safe Person," how do you handle a delayed text? You probably don't even notice it. Your brain doesn't interpret their silence as a "System Failure." It interprets it as "They're probably just busy." That is the code you need.

Highlight and Copy: The next time you feel an Anxious Loop or an Avoidant Shutdown starting with a partner or a parent, pause. Access the "Secure" file. Ask yourself: How would I react to this exact situation if it were my best friend doing it?

Execute the Paste: This is the hard part. It requires you to ignore the "Malware" of your old survival scripts and choose the "Secure" response instead. If your Secure Code says "Silence is neutral," then you force yourself to put the phone down and wait, rather than sending the "Signal Test" text.

RE-ROUTING THE SIGNAL

You are essentially building a bridge between servers. By consciously bringing the calm, steady logic of your friendships into the "Hotspots" of your dating life or family dynamics, you are re-routing the signal.

Every time you choose a "Secure" response over an "Anxious" or "Avoidant" one, you are overwriting the old, buggy code. You are teaching your nervous system that it doesn't need to "Crash" to stay safe. You are realizing that you have the Admin Rights to decide which version of you shows up to the conversation.

You are not a victim of your "Default Settings." You are the Lead Developer of your own heart, and you have the power to upgrade the interface whenever you choose.

THE CODE-BREAKER EXERCISE: AUDITING YOUR SECURE BASELINE

Before you can Copy-Paste your security, you have to find the "Clean Code" in your system. This exercise is a deep-dive audit of the places where your signal is already strong, steady, and glitch-free.

Grab your phone or a notebook. We're going to look for the "Safe Networks" you already inhabit but might be taking for granted.

Step 1: Identify Your "Low-Latency" Connection

Think of one person in your life—a best friend, a sibling, a mentor, or even a long-term coworker—with whom you feel zero pressure.

When they don't text back for six hours, what is your immediate thought? (e.g., "They're probably napping" vs. "They hate me").

When you make a mistake around them, do you feel the need to "Delete the History" or "Re-write the Narrative"? Or do you just let it be?

Do you feel like you have to keep your "Firewall" up, or can you leave the front door open?

The Goal: This person is your Reference Server. The way you feel with them is what "Secure" actually feels like in your nervous system. Write their name down.

Step 2: Deconstruct the Secure Script

Now, let's look at the "Metadata" of that relationship. Why does it work?

The Silence Test: How long can you go without a "Ping" from them before you feel anxious? (Is it days? Weeks?).

The Conflict Log: When you have a disagreement, do you "System Crash" (Fearful-Avoidant), "Shutdown" (Avoidant), or "Hyper-activate" (Anxious)? Or do you just... talk about it?

The Vulnerability Level: On a scale of 1 to 10, how "Peeled" do you feel when you tell them something personal? Does it feel like a "Security Breach" or just a "Data Sync"?

Step 3: Extract the "Clean Code"

Look at your answers. You've just identified a version of yourself that is Secure.

Your "Secure Code" for silence is: "Distance is not Disconnection."

Your "Secure Code" for mistakes is: "I am allowed to be human."

Your "Secure Code" for vulnerability is: "Being seen is safe."

Step 4: The Manual Override (The Hack)

Now, think of the "Dead Zone" in your life—the relationship where you are currently glitching (the Anxious date, the Avoidant parent).

The Trigger: They haven't texted back in two hours. Your "Anxious Malware" is trying to run a "Panic.exe" script.

The Code-Break: Pause. Open the file from your Reference Server (Step 1).

The Command: Ask yourself, "If [Safe Person's Name] hadn't texted me back in two hours, would I care?"

The Execute: Use the Safe Person's Script instead of the Panic Script. Force your brain to run the "They're just busy" code.

The Reality Check:

Your brain will fight this. It will tell you that the "Date" is different from the "Friend." It will tell you the stakes are higher, so the "Firewall" must stay up. But the Code-Breaker is designed to remind you that your nervous system is capable of peace. You aren't learning a new trick; you're just re-routing the traffic from a high-speed server to a buggy one.

THE FIREWALL AUDIT: IDENTIFYING YOUR DEFENSIVE ENCRYPTION

While the Code-Breaker is for finding your security, the Firewall Audit is for those who default to Avoidant or Fearful-Avoidant (Disorganized) patterns. If your "Survival Mode" is to go "Airplane Mode" or "Shutdown" when things get too real, you aren't just being "independent"—you're running a high-level security protocol to prevent a perceived Data Breach.

To stop the "Glitch," you have to understand the Architecture of your Defense.

Step 1: Locate the "Encryption" Trigger

Think of a recent moment when you felt the "Snap." Maybe a friend asked an "Honest Question," or a partner wanted a "Marathon of Exposure" (a deep talk).

The Physical Signal: Did your chest feel laced tight by an invisible cord? Did you feel a sudden, urgent need to check your email or "Be Busy"?

The Internal Log: What was the first thought that hit the server? (e.g., "They're trapping me," "This is too much," or "I need to leave before they see the flaw.")

The Goal: This is your Auto-Defense Script. Your brain is treating a "Connection Request" as a "Malware Attack."

Step 2: Deconstruct the "Load-Bearing Walls"

Why did you build this specific wall? Look at the "Metadata" of your history.

The Origin Code: When was the first time being "Seen" led to a "System Failure"? (e.g., were you judged, smothered, or let down?).

The False Logic: What lie is the Firewall telling you right now? (e.g., "If I stay 'Offline,' I can't be deleted," or "If I show them the basement, they'll leave anyway.")

Step 3: Test the "Permissions"

Look at the person you are currently pushing away. Are they actually a threat, or are they just a Secure Signal you don't know how to process?

The Permission Check: Have they ever actually "hacked" you? Have they used your secrets as weapons, or have they stayed consistent even when you were "Glitching"?

The Buffer Test: What would happen if you lowered the Firewall by just 1%? What if you sent a "Status Update" like, "I'm feeling a bit overwhelmed, but I'm still here," instead of just "Going Dark"?

Step 4: The Manual Override (The Admin Access)

The next time the Serrated Hum of the phone makes you want to retreat into your bunker:

The Pause: Acknowledge the Firewall. "My system is trying to go into Airplane Mode right now."

The Access Request: Open your Reference Server from the Code-Breaker. Remember how it feels to be "Visible" with your Safe Person.

The Command: Force yourself to stay in the "Chat." Don't "Delete the Contact." Don't "Move to a different state." Just stay on the line for five more minutes.

The Reality Check:

For the Avoidant-leaning heart, safety feels like danger. Staying "Seen" feels like standing under a spotlight with no clothes. But the Firewall Audit reminds you that the bunker is a lonely place to live. By identifying your "Load-Bearing Walls," you can finally decide which ones are actually keeping the roof up—and which ones are just keeping the "Strong Signal" out.

MY ATTACHMENT MAP

Now that you've audited your code and inspected your firewalls, it's time to visualize your personal network. This map is designed to show you that you aren't a static point on a graph; you are a shifting signal.

Fill out this map to see where your "Strongest Connection" lives and where you're currently experiencing "No Service."

Use this System Status Log to audit your internal network. For each "Territory" below, identify your current Operating System (Secure, Anxious, Avoidant, or Fearful-Avoidant), your most common Auto-Reply, and your Signal Strength (1–5 bars).

1. Territory: Best Friends

Operating System: ____________________

My Auto-Reply: (e.g., "I'm here if you need to talk," or "Checking in on you.")

Signal Strength: [1] [2] [3] [4] [5]

The Connection: Do you trust the link is stable even when they are "Offline"?

2. Territory: Dating & Romance

Operating System: ____________________

My Auto-Reply: (e.g., "Why haven't you texted back?" or "I think we should take a break.")

Signal Strength: [1] [2] [3] [4] [5]

The Connection: Does the "Space between the Sent and the Reply" feel like a "Network Error"?

3. Territory: Family (Parents/Siblings)

Operating System: ____________________

My Auto-Reply: (e.g., "I'm just busy. Talk later," or "Everything's fine.")

Signal Strength: [1] [2] [3] [4] [5]

The Connection: Are you reacting to the "Original Code" or the person you are today?

4. Territory: Work & School

Operating System: ______________________

My Auto-Reply: (e.g., "I've got this under control," or "Sorry, I'm swamped.")

Signal Strength: [1] [2] [3] [4] [5]

The Connection: Is your "Secure Signal" here based on your skill set or your fear of being seen as "Broken"?

5. Territory: Social Media & Online

Operating System: ______________________

My Auto-Reply: (e.g., Ghosting, over-sharing, or "Blocking" when things get too real.)

Signal Strength: [1] [2] [3] [4] [5]

The Connection: Is your "Profile" a true reflection of the "Signal" you want to send?

ANALYZING THE DEAD ZONES

Review your System Status Log above. The areas where your "Bars" are lowest are your Dead Zones. These are the territories where your old survival scripts have hijacked the interface.

The High-Latency Territory: Which relationship makes you feel the most Anxious (constantly searching for service)? What is the specific "Ping" (a text, a look, a silence) that triggers your need to verify the link?

My Trigger:

____

The Firewall Territory: Which relationship makes you feel the most Avoidant (wanting to go into Airplane Mode)? What is the "Security Breach" you are trying to prevent by staying unreachable?

The Breach I Fear:

____

The System Crash Territory: In which relationship do you feel Fearful-Avoidant (wanting to run toward and away at the same time)? What does the "Serrated Hum" of their name on your screen feel like in your body?

The Physical Sensation:

____

THE "COPY-PASTE" PLAN

Identify your Reference Server—the relationship where you have 5 bars of Secure Signal.

The Secure Script: Write down one thing you do in your Secure relationship that you never do in your "Dead Zone." (e.g., "I tell them when I'm having a bad day without worrying they'll leave.")

My Secure Script:

____

The Manual Override: This week, pick one "Dead Zone" relationship. When you feel the "Glitch" coming on, force your system to run the Secure Script instead.

My Action Item:

____

THE INTERNAL AUDIT: WHAT THE MAP REVEALS

Take a second to look at your System Status Log. It's likely a patchwork of different signals—a 5-bar connection with your best friend, a "Searching for Service" glitch in your romantic life, and perhaps a "Firewall Active" warning when your parents call.

This is the most important lesson of Chapter 9: You are not your glitches.

If you were truly "broken," you wouldn't have a Reference Server. You wouldn't have any 5-bar connections at all. The fact that you can be secure in one territory is proof that the code exists. It's not missing; it's just not being routed to every department yet.

<u>WHY THE SIGNAL DROPS</u>

- When you see a "Dead Zone" on your map, don't judge it. Understand it.

- The Interference: Sometimes the person on the other end is sending a "Noisy Signal" that makes it impossible for you to stay Secure.

- The Legacy Hardware: Sometimes you are trying to run a new, healthy relationship on an old, traumatic server that hasn't been updated since you were ten years old.

- The Bandwidth Limit: Sometimes life is just too heavy, and your system has defaulted to "Power-Save Mode" to keep you from crashing.

THE ADMIN'S FINAL WORD

Attachment is not a cage; it is a Context. You are the one who decides which "Apps" run and which "Signals" you prioritize. You are the architect of the connection.

When you find yourself "Glitching" at a dinner table or spiraling over a text at 11:00 PM, remember the person who was "Secure" at 2:00 PM. That version of you isn't gone; they just aren't logged in right now. Your job is to learn how to Sync the Servers.

Stop asking, "Why am I like this?" and start asking, "Which network am I on right now, and do I have the Admin Rights to change the settings?"

"In the next chapter, we move beyond the map. We're going to look at how Safety Rewires Patterns and why Awareness is Power. It's time to learn the Manual Overrides you need to stay 'Online' when it matters most, remembering that in this interface, Growth ≠ Perfection.

Chapter 10:

HARD RESET: MOVING BEYOND FACTORY SETTINGS

The previous chapters of your life may have been written by others — the caregivers who were inconsistent, the partners who reinforced your fears, or the circumstances that taught you that closeness was a gamble. These experiences shaped how you learned to connect, how you learned to protect yourself, and how you learned to expect love.

But Chapter 10 is where you take the pen back.

Here, we move from the archaeology of your past to the architecture of your future. We begin shifting from understanding why you became who you are... to consciously deciding who you want to become.

One of the most hopeful discoveries in modern psychology is that attachment is not fixed. Your attachment style is not a life sentence. It is a pattern — one that formed through experience and can be reshaped through new experience.

This process is known as Earned Secure Attachment.

Earned security does not come from a perfect childhood. It does not require flawless relationships or complete emotional healing. Instead, it develops through the conscious work of adulthood — through awareness, safer experiences, and the gradual rewiring of how you relate to yourself and others.

It is the security that is built, not given. The safety that is learned, not assumed. The stability that emerges when you refuse to let your history dictate your future.

And this is where real change begins.

SAFETY REWIRES PATTERNS: THE BIOLOGY OF CHANGE

We often think of safety as a concept — or simply the absence of conflict. No arguments. No tension. No distance.

But safety is not just what isn't happening. Safety is something your body feels.

In reality, safety is an active, biological signal. Your nervous system is a living record of every time you weren't heard, protected, or seen. Every experience of unpredictability, distance, or emotional inconsistency leaves an imprint. Over time, these imprints shape how you respond to closeness, vulnerability, and connection.

If love once felt uncertain, your body learned to stay alert. If closeness led to disappointment, your body learned to brace for loss.

If vulnerability was met with distance, your body learned to protect itself.

These patterns were not conscious decisions. They were adaptations.

Your nervous system learned what it needed to survive.

The challenge is that these records are not erased by logic. You cannot simply tell yourself that things are different now and expect your body to believe it. These patterns are not rewritten through understanding alone — they are rewritten through experience.

Healing happens when your nervous system begins to encounter something new.

Consistency instead of unpredictability.

Calm instead of tension.

Presence instead of distance.

Over time, these experiences begin to overwrite the old patterns. The nervous system slowly learns that closeness does not always lead to pain, that vulnerability does not always lead to rejection, and that connection can exist without fear.

This is how safety rewires patterns.

Not through perfection.

Not through forcing yourself to change.

But through repeated experiences that teach your body something new:

It is safe to connect.

It is safe to stay.

It is safe to be seen.

And when your nervous system begins to believe that... everything starts to change.

THE NEUROPLASTICITY OF TRUST

For decades, psychologists believed the brain was largely fixed by adulthood — that the patterns formed in childhood would define how we relate to others for the rest of our lives. Today, we know the brain remains capable of change throughout life.

This ability is known as neuroplasticity — the brain's capacity to form new neural pathways based on new experiences.

If your early life taught you that closeness equals pain, your brain built a fast, efficient pathway to that conclusion. Over time, that pathway becomes automatic. When someone gets close, your nervous system reacts quickly — not necessarily because danger is present, but because danger was present before.

Your brain learned to protect you.

The more often that pattern repeated, the stronger the pathway became. Like a well-traveled road, it became easier and faster to follow, even when it no longer served you.

Healing involves building a new road.

This process does not happen through thinking alone. Insight is helpful, but experience is what creates change. Your nervous system needs to encounter something different — moments where closeness does not lead to pain, where vulnerability is met with steadiness, and where connection feels safe instead of uncertain.

This is where co-regulation becomes essential.

Co-regulation is the process where the calm nervous system of another person — a partner, a friend, or a therapist — helps stabilize your own. When someone responds with patience instead of withdrawal, or consistency instead of unpredictability, your nervous system begins to settle.

When you repeatedly experience being seen without being judged... heard without being dismissed... and soothed without being overwhelmed... your brain begins to shift.

Old "danger" pathways start to weaken. New "connection" pathways begin to strengthen.

Over time, your nervous system learns something new:

Closeness does not always lead to pain. Vulnerability does not always lead to rejection. Connection can feel safe.

Trust, then, is not simply a decision. It is something your nervous system learns—slowly, gradually, and through experience.

And with enough of those experiences, the road that once led to fear begins to lead somewhere different.

SAFETY IS SENSED, NOT BELIEVED

Safety is not simply a thought. It is a physiological shift.

You can tell yourself that someone is trustworthy, that a relationship is healthy, or that things are different now — but your nervous system does not change through logic alone. It changes through experience.

As described in polyvagal theory, developed by Dr. Stephen Porges, safety occurs when the nervous system shifts out of protection mode and into connection mode. When you feel unsafe, your body prepares for threat — your heart rate increases, your muscles tense, and your mind scans for danger. This is the sympathetic nervous system activating to protect you.

When you feel safe, a different system takes over — often referred to as the social engagement system. In this state, your body softens, your breathing slows, and connection becomes easier. Curiosity replaces vigilance. Openness replaces defensiveness.

This is not something you force. It is something you feel.

You cannot argue yourself into safety. You must experience it.

Safety often looks subtle and quiet. It may appear in moments such as:

The Physical Release

You notice your shoulders drop. Your breathing deepens. Your jaw unclenches. Your body softens in the presence of someone specific.

The Emotional Anchor

You sense that even if you make a mistake, the relationship will not suddenly disappear. There is room for imperfection without fear of abandonment.

The Environment of Low Stakes

You find yourself around people who prioritize being with you rather than fixing you. You feel accepted without needing to perform, explain, or defend yourself.

These moments may feel unfamiliar at first. In fact, safety can sometimes feel uncomfortable if your nervous system is used to intensity, unpredictability, or emotional distance. Calm can feel unfamiliar when your body has learned to expect tension.

But when these experiences happen consistently, your nervous system begins to recognize something new.

The body starts to believe what the mind already hopes:

It is safe to be me.

It is safe to stay.

It is safe to be with you.

And as this belief settles into the body, your patterns begin to shift — not through force, but through experience.

AWARENESS IS POWER: THE ARCHITECTURE OF CHOICE

If safety is the soil, awareness is the light.

Safety creates the conditions for change, but awareness is what allows growth to take root. You cannot change a pattern you cannot see. Until you recognize your responses, they remain automatic— shaping your relationships without your conscious participation.

Most attachment behaviors develop as adaptive strategies. Clinging when we sense distance, withdrawing when things begin to feel too close, overanalyzing small shifts in tone, or creating emotional distance before someone else can — these patterns were not random. They were learned in response to experiences that once felt overwhelming, unpredictable, or unsafe.

At one point, these responses protected you.

They helped you avoid rejection.

They helped you manage uncertainty.

They helped you maintain connection in the ways that felt possible at the time.

They were once your armor.

But over time, what once protected you can begin to limit you. The same strategies that helped you survive earlier experiences may now prevent deeper connection, emotional safety, and growth.

What once felt like protection can begin to feel like restriction.

Your armor becomes your cage.

Awareness is what creates the opening.

When you begin to notice your patterns — the urge to pull away, the need for reassurance, the instinct to overinterpret silence — you create space between feeling and reaction. That space is where choice becomes possible.

Instead of reacting automatically, you begin to respond intentionally.

And in that moment, change begins.

FROM "AUTOMATIC" TO "CONSCIOUS"

Insecure patterns are often hidden in plain sight because they are automatic. They happen quickly, often before you fully recognize what you are feeling. A delayed reply, a shift in tone, or a moment of emotional closeness can trigger responses that feel immediate and instinctive.

You may find yourself pulling away without fully understanding why.

You may feel the urge to seek reassurance before you consciously recognize the anxiety beneath it.

You may begin to overanalyze, withdraw, or protect yourself — all before you realize what has been activated.

These reactions are not intentional. They are learned responses shaped by past experiences.

When awareness develops, something subtle but important begins to shift. Instead of moving straight from trigger to reaction, you begin to notice what is happening as it unfolds.

You might recognize the tightening in your chest before you withdraw.

You might notice the urge to send another message before acting on it.

You might become aware of the story forming in your mind before it feels like truth.

This awareness creates a pause.

That pause may only last a few seconds, but it changes the experience. Instead of reacting automatically, you begin to observe your internal state with curiosity rather than urgency.

You may find yourself thinking, *I'm feeling the urge to push them away right now because I'm afraid of being rejected later.* Or, *I notice I'm becoming anxious because they haven't responded, and my mind is starting to create a story.*

This shift does not eliminate the feeling, but it changes your relationship to it. The impulse is still present, but it no longer feels like the only option.

You begin to recognize that what you are feeling is a familiar pattern—not necessarily a reflection of the present moment.

Over time, this awareness softens the intensity of automatic reactions. What once felt immediate and overwhelming begins to feel more manageable. You gain the ability to sit with discomfort, to observe rather than immediately respond, and to move through moments that once triggered stronger reactions.

This is how awareness gradually transforms automatic patterns into conscious responses — not all at once, but through repeated moments of noticing, pausing, and choosing differently.

THE "NAME IT TO TAME IT" EFFECT

Psychiatrist Dr. Dan Siegel coined the phrase *"name it to tame it."* When we put words to our internal state, we begin to calm the nervous system. Research suggests that labeling emotions shifts activity from the emotional centers of the brain—particularly the amygdala—to areas involved in reasoning and regulation, such as the prefrontal cortex.

In simple terms, when you name what you are feeling, you create space between the emotion and your response.

Instead of being overwhelmed by a feeling, you begin to understand it.

Instead of reacting automatically, you begin to regulate.

This is why awareness is not just helpful—it is transformative.

To build this awareness, you must become familiar with your own patterns. Over time, you begin to notice the signals that appear when your attachment system is activated. These signals often show up as subtle physical sensations, emotional shifts, or familiar thought patterns.

These are your "tells."

The Anxious Tell

A racing heart. A sudden need to know where someone is or what they are thinking. An urge to send another message. An obsessive replay of a conversation, searching for signs of distance or rejection.

The Avoidant Tell

A feeling of numbness. A sudden focus on a partner's flaws. A sense of needing space without fully understanding why. A physical desire to leave the room or emotionally withdraw when closeness increases.

The Disorganized Tell

A sense of being frozen or overwhelmed. A confusing mix of wanting to be close while feeling afraid. Shifting quickly between seeking reassurance and pushing someone away.

These responses are not flaws. They are signals.

Awareness is not about judging these feelings or trying to eliminate them. Instead, it is about recognizing them as information. They are reminders of past experiences, not necessarily reflections of the present moment.

When you begin to see your patterns this way, something important shifts. What once felt overwhelming begins to feel understandable. What once felt urgent begins to feel manageable.

You begin to recognize your reactions as data from the past— not truth about the present.

And with that understanding, your relationship to these feelings begins to change.

Growth ≠ Perfection: The Reality of the Journey

One of the most common—and most harmful—myths in healing is the belief that becoming secure means becoming perfect.

It doesn't.

Securely attached people still get triggered. They still feel jealous, uncertain, or overwhelmed at times. They still have moments where old fears surface or emotions feel bigger than expected. Growth does not eliminate these experiences.

What changes is how they move through them.

Security is not defined by the absence of conflict. It is defined by the presence of repair.

Securely attached individuals still experience misunderstandings, emotional distance, and difficult conversations. The difference is that these moments no longer feel like the end of the relationship. Instead, they become opportunities to reconnect, clarify, and rebuild.

In insecure attachment patterns, conflict often feels threatening. A disagreement may trigger fears of abandonment, rejection, or emotional distance. These fears can lead to withdrawal, defensiveness, or attempts to regain control.

With growing security, conflict begins to feel different. It becomes something that can be navigated rather than avoided. Discomfort becomes tolerable. Repair becomes possible.

Growth, then, is not about never struggling. It is about learning that struggle does not have to lead to disconnection.

This shift is subtle but powerful. Instead of expecting relationships to remain perfect, you begin to trust that connection can survive imperfection.

And that is where lasting security begins to take shape.

THE MYTH OF THE "HEALED" DESTINATION

Perfectionism often develops as a response to uncertainty and emotional pain. If being imperfect once led to rejection, criticism, or distance, it makes sense that you might begin striving to be "good enough" in ways that feel safer. Over time, this can turn into a quiet belief: if I do everything right, I won't be hurt again.

But healing does not work that way.

Growth is not linear. It is uneven, layered, and sometimes unpredictable. There will be days when you fall back into old habits. Moments when you overthink, seek reassurance, withdraw, or protect yourself in familiar ways. These experiences are not signs that you have failed. They are part of the process.

Growth is not the absence of these moments.

It is the speed of your recovery.

How quickly can you notice that you've drifted into an old pattern?
How gently can you bring yourself back?

How willing are you to reconnect instead of retreat?

These questions shift the focus away from perfection and toward progress.

THE 30% RULE AND THE POWER OF REPAIR

Research into infant attachment suggests that caregivers only need to be attuned to a child's needs about 30% of the time for secure attachment to develop. The remaining 70% consists of misattunements—moments where needs are missed, misunderstood, or delayed—followed by repair.

Security is not built through perfection. It is built through repair.

This same principle applies to adult relationships and personal growth. You do not need to respond perfectly every time. You do not need to avoid every trigger or handle every moment flawlessly. What matters most is your willingness to return, reconnect, and repair.

This is what growth looks like in practice:

Acknowledging the Rupture

"I realized I shut down earlier when we were talking."

Taking Responsibility

"I was feeling overwhelmed, and I took it out on you."

Re-establishing Connection

"Can we try that conversation again?"

These moments of repair build trust — not just with others, but within yourself. Each time you return instead of retreating, your nervous system learns something new: disconnection does not have to be permanent.

Over time, this changes how you experience relationships. Conflict becomes less threatening. Misunderstandings become more manageable. Connection begins to feel more stable, even when things are imperfect.

And this is how security develops — not through getting everything right, but through learning how to find your way back.

SELF-COMPASSION AS FUEL

Attachment wounds often run deep, which means the healing process can feel especially vulnerable. When old patterns surface, it can be tempting to respond with self-criticism — to judge yourself for reacting, overthinking, or falling back into familiar behaviors. Yet self-criticism tends to reactivate the very threat system you are trying to calm.

When you judge yourself harshly, your nervous system interprets that judgment as danger. The body tightens. Defensiveness rises. Learning becomes harder. Instead of creating space for growth, self-criticism reinforces the same protective patterns you are trying to move beyond.

Self-compassion works differently.

Self-compassion does not mean ignoring mistakes or avoiding responsibility. It means responding to yourself with the same understanding you might offer someone else who is trying to change. It allows you to recognize when you have slipped into old patterns without turning that moment into evidence that you are failing.

Growth often requires a bias toward action — the willingness to try again, even when the outcome is uncertain. Self-compassion makes this possible. When you know you can return to yourself without harsh judgment, you become more willing to take emotional risks, to communicate more openly, and to attempt new ways of responding.

This might look like:

Noticing you became anxious and choosing to pause instead of sending another message.

Recognizing you withdrew and deciding to reconnect later. Acknowledging you overreacted and offering yourself patience while you repair.

These moments are small, but they build momentum. Each time you respond to yourself with compassion instead of criticism, you create an environment where growth becomes more sustainable.

You cannot shame yourself into becoming someone you love.

But you can support yourself into becoming someone you trust.

And over time, that trust becomes the foundation for lasting change.

Before you move forward, take a moment to reflect on what you've learned in this chapter. Safety, awareness, and growth are not ideas to understand once — they are patterns to practice over time. The following worksheet is designed to help you begin applying these concepts in your own life, at your own pace. There is no rush. Growth happens through small moments of noticing, repairing, and returning.

CHAPTER 10 WORKSHEET

HARD RESET: MOVING BEYOND FACTORY SETTINGS

This worksheet is designed to help you begin noticing your patterns, recognizing moments of growth, and practicing repair. There are no right or wrong answers. This is about awareness, not perfection.

PART I: RECOGNIZING SAFETY

Think about moments when you feel most at ease in relationships.

1. When do I feel safest in connection with others?

____

____

____

2. What behaviors from others help me feel calm and secure?

Examples may include consistency, listening, patience, reassurance, or emotional presence.

3. How does my body feel when I experience safety?

Examples: relaxed shoulders, slower breathing, feeling calm, less overthinking.

PART II: BECOMING AWARE OF MY PATTERNS

Everyone has attachment "tells." These are the signals that appear when your attachment system is activated.

1. My anxious tells might include:

2. My avoidant tells might include:

3. When I feel triggered, I tend to:

☐ Seek reassurance

☐ Withdraw

☐ Overthink

☐ Become defensive

☐ Shut down

☐ Other: ________________________________

____

PART III: GROWTH WITHOUT PERFECTION

Growth is not about never falling into old patterns. It is about noticing and returning.

1. A recent moment where I noticed an old pattern:

____

____

____

2. What did I do next?

____

____

____

3. If I could revisit that moment with more awareness, I might:

____

____

____

PART IV: PRACTICING REPAIR

Repair is one of the most powerful tools for building secure attachment.

Complete the following:

1. A conversation or interaction I may want to repair:

____

____

____

2. What I might say to acknowledge the rupture:

____

____

____

3. How I might reconnect:

____

____

____

PART V: SELF-COMPASSION REFLECTION

1. When I fall into old patterns, I usually tell myself:

2. A more compassionate response I could offer myself:

3. One way I can practice self-compassion this week:

CLOSING REFLECTION

Growth does not happen all at once. It develops through small moments of awareness, repair, and compassion.

What is one small shift I want to practice moving forward?

Chapter 11:

OVERRIDE THE DEFAULTS

By now, you may have started to recognize your patterns.

You may see yourself in the anxious pull toward reassurance.

The avoidant urge to withdraw.

The disorganized push and pull between closeness and distance.

For some readers, this realization brings clarity. For others, it brings something heavier — a quiet fear that these patterns define who you are.

This is where we pause.

Because this is not what attachment theory is meant to do.

Attachment styles are not identities.

They are not diagnoses.

They are not personality flaws.

They are patterns.

And patterns can change.

If earlier chapters helped you recognize your "default settings," this chapter is about understanding something just as important:

Defaults are not destiny.

You were shaped by your experiences, but you are not limited to them.

You adapted in the ways that made survival possible.

You learned to love in the ways that felt safest.

There was wisdom in those adaptations.

There was intelligence in those responses.

But survival strategies are not meant to be permanent settings.

They are meant to evolve.

NOT A DIAGNOSIS

One of the most common misunderstandings about attachment styles is the belief that they function like diagnoses.

They do not.

Attachment patterns are fluid.

They shift across relationships, life stages, and experiences.

You may feel secure with one person and anxious with another.
You may feel avoidant during stress and open during stability.
You may find yourself moving between patterns as you grow.

This is not inconsistency.

This is humanity.

Attachment styles describe tendencies, not fixed identities. They reflect how your nervous system learned to respond to closeness, distance, and emotional risk.

And like any learned response, they can be unlearned.

When we treat attachment styles as diagnoses, we risk creating a new form of limitation:

"I'm anxious, so I'll always be this way."

"I'm avoidant, so I can't handle closeness."

"I'm disorganized, so relationships will always be chaotic."

These beliefs quietly remove your agency.

They turn patterns into permanence.

But attachment theory was never meant to confine you.

It was meant to free you.

NOT A PERSONALITY FLAW

There is another subtle danger in learning about attachment styles: shame.

When readers recognize anxious or avoidant patterns, they often begin to judge themselves.

Why am I like this?

Why do I overthink everything?

Why do I push people away?

These questions carry an assumption: that something is wrong with you.

But attachment patterns are not flaws.

They are adaptations.

If you became anxious, you likely learned that connection was inconsistent.

You adapted by staying alert, attuned, and vigilant.

If you became avoidant, you likely learned that closeness felt overwhelming or unreliable.

You adapted by becoming self-sufficient and emotionally guarded.

If your pattern became disorganized, you likely experienced closeness as both comforting and unsafe. You adapted by moving between approach and retreat.

These are not weaknesses.

They are intelligent responses to emotional environments.

Your nervous system did not malfunction.

It protected you.

And now, as your life evolves, those same strategies may no longer serve you in the same way.

This is not failure.

This is growth.

NOT SOMETHING TO WEAPONIZE

Another risk in learning attachment styles is using them to define — or limit — others.

You may begin to recognize patterns in partners, friends, or people from your past.

You might think:

"They're avoidant."

"They're anxious."

"They're disorganized."

While this awareness can be helpful, it becomes harmful when used as a label rather than a lens.

Attachment theory is not meant to categorize people. It is meant to increase compassion.

When labels become fixed, they create distance instead of understanding.

"They're avoidant" can quietly become:

"They don't care."

"They can't change."

"They'll always hurt me."

But people are not static systems.

They are adaptive, evolving, and shaped by experience.

Attachment theory is meant to create empathy—not certainty.

It helps us understand behavior, not define identity.

When used with care, attachment awareness softens judgment.

It allows us to see fear where we once saw rejection. Protection where we once saw indifference.

Uncertainty where we once saw disinterest.

This is where understanding becomes compassion.

DEFAULTS CAN BE OVERRIDDEN

If attachment patterns were learned, they can be reshaped.

This is the quiet hope beneath everything you have read so far.

You are not locked into your early experiences.

You are not bound to the way you first learned to love.

You are allowed to grow.

You are allowed to personalize your settings.

Overriding the defaults rarely happens in dramatic moments.

It happens quietly, in small decisions that feel almost invisible at first.

It might look like pausing before sending a message you would have once sent in panic.

It might look like staying present during a difficult conversation instead of withdrawing.

It might look like asking for reassurance instead of pretending you do not need it.

These moments are subtle, but they represent something profound.

You are interrupting automatic responses.

You are creating space between feeling and reaction. You are allowing yourself to choose differently.

At first, this can feel uncomfortable.

New patterns often do.

Your nervous system is used to familiar responses, even when they create distance or pain.

When you begin responding differently, it may feel unnatural, uncertain, or even unsafe.

This does not mean you are doing it wrong.

It means you are learning something new.

You may notice yourself wanting to withdraw, but choosing to stay.

You may feel the urge to overanalyze, but choosing to trust.

You may feel fear rising, but choosing to communicate instead of shutting down.

These are the quiet moments where change begins.

Over time, these choices accumulate.

What once felt uncomfortable begins to feel familiar.

What once felt risky begins to feel safe.

What once felt impossible begins to feel natural.

This is how new attachment patterns develop.

Not through perfection.

Not through sudden transformation.

But through repetition, awareness, and gentle correction.

You are not replacing who you are.

You are expanding how you relate.

You are not erasing your past.

You are allowing your future to look different.

This is what it means to override the defaults.

PERSONALIZING THE SETTINGS

Once you begin overriding the defaults, something important begins to happen.

You stop reacting based on fear, and start responding based on intention.

You begin to personalize the way you connect.

You may discover that you need more reassurance than you once allowed yourself to ask for.

You may realize that you need more space than you once believed was acceptable.

You may learn that healthy relationships allow for both closeness and independence.

This is where attachment becomes less about categories and more about awareness.

You are no longer asking,

"Am I anxious?"

"Am I avoidant?"

"Am I disorganized?"

You are asking,

"What do I need right now?"

"What helps me feel safe?"

"What supports connection without losing myself?"

This shift is subtle, but powerful.

You move from identifying with patterns to shaping them.

You move from reacting automatically to responding intentionally.

You move from inherited settings to personalized ones.

There is no single version of secure attachment. There is only the version that feels safe, balanced, and authentic to you.

This is where your way of loving begins to evolve.

Not by abandoning who you are, but by allowing yourself to grow beyond the ways you once had to survive.

<u>MINI-EXERCISE</u>

Labels I Refuse to Wear

Take a moment to reflect on any labels you may have assigned to yourself.

Complete the following:

Labels I have used to define myself:

____

____

____

Where did I learn these labels?

____

____

____

How might these labels have limited me?

____

____

____

Now, consider replacing these labels with something more flexible:

Instead of "I am anxious,"

I might say:

"I sometimes feel anxious when connection feels uncertain."

Instead of "I am avoidant,"

I might say:

"I sometimes withdraw when closeness feels overwhelming."

Instead of "I am disorganized,"

I might say:

"I sometimes feel conflicted between closeness and safety."

Now write your own reframed statements:

You are not your defaults.

You are not your past.

You are not the first way you learned to love.

You adapted.

You survived.

And now, you are allowed to personalize the settings.

Quietly.

Gradually.

In your own time.

PART IV:
Closing

By now, something has shifted. You may not feel entirely different, and you may still notice familiar reactions or old patterns emerging in moments of stress or uncertainty. But there is a new awareness forming beneath those responses. You are beginning to notice what once felt automatic. You are pausing where you once reacted. You are starting to choose differently.

The way you learned to love was shaped by your experiences. You adapted to closeness that felt uncertain, distance that felt safer, and connection that sometimes brought both comfort and fear. These patterns were not mistakes. They were intelligent responses to the environments you moved through. They helped you survive when safety and consistency were not guaranteed.

But survival is not the same as living. As you move forward, the focus begins to shift from understanding your patterns to shaping them. This is where growth becomes more personal. You begin to override the defaults and explore what connection looks like when it is guided by intention rather than fear.

There is no single way to do this. You begin to personalize the settings, discovering what safety feels like for you, what closeness means for you, and how connection can exist without losing yourself. This next section invites you into that space — where the way you learned to love begins to evolve, quietly and gradually, in your own time.

Chapter 12:

PERSONALIZING THE SETTINGS

LEARNING TO LOVE WITH AWARENESS INSTEAD OF FEAR

At the beginning of this journey, the space between replies may have felt heavy with meaning. Silence may have felt like distance. Closeness may have felt uncertain. You may have found yourself searching for reassurance, pulling away to protect yourself, or moving between connection and fear without fully understanding why.

Now, that space may begin to feel different — not empty, but calm. Not uncertain, but open. The urgency that once surrounded connection may begin to soften. The fear that once shaped your reactions may loosen its grip. The space between closeness and distance may begin to feel easier to navigate.

At some point in this journey, you may begin to notice that relationships feel different. Not perfect, and not without moments of uncertainty, but quieter. The urgency that once surrounded connection may begin to soften. The fear that once shaped your reactions may loosen its grip.

These changes often emerge gradually. You may pause before reacting in situations that once felt overwhelming. You may express what you are feeling instead of withdrawing. You may allow closeness without immediately preparing yourself for loss. These shifts are subtle, but they represent something meaningful. You are no longer responding solely from what you learned in the past. You are responding from who you are becoming.

Old patterns may still surface from time to time. You may still feel anxious when someone becomes distant, or feel the urge to withdraw when closeness feels vulnerable. The difference is not the absence of these reactions, but the awareness that now accompanies them. You may notice your response more quickly. You may offer yourself compassion instead of judgment. You may pause long enough to choose a different path.

Growth rarely happens in dramatic moments. More often, it unfolds quietly through repeated experiences of awareness and intention. Conversations may begin to feel calmer. Silence may no longer feel threatening. Closeness may feel less overwhelming and more sustainable. Trust may develop slowly, but with greater steadiness. Connection may begin to feel less fragile and more secure.

As these changes take shape, the relationship you have with yourself often begins to shift as well. You may start to trust your reactions instead of questioning them. You may recognize your needs without viewing them as weaknesses. You may allow yourself to ask for reassurance, take space when necessary, or move toward connection without fear of losing yourself.

The way you learned to love shaped how you moved through connection. It influenced how you responded to closeness, distance, and vulnerability. Those patterns helped you navigate uncertainty and protect yourself when safety was not guaranteed. But those patterns were never meant to remain fixed. They were shaped by your experiences, and as your experiences change, so can the way you relate.

Personalizing the settings means allowing yourself to move beyond inherited patterns. It means recognizing that you are not limited to the ways you once learned to connect. Instead, you begin to define what safety feels like for you, what boundaries support your well-being, and what closeness looks like when it is guided by intention rather than fear.

This process does not happen all at once. It unfolds gradually, through small moments of awareness and choice. Each time you respond with intention instead of reaction, you reinforce a new pattern. Each time you approach yourself with compassion instead of judgment, you deepen your growth.

Over time, relationships may begin to feel more balanced and less driven by fear. You may feel more grounded in connection and more comfortable with both closeness and independence. You may begin to experience a quieter form of trust — one that builds gradually and does not require constant reassurance.

You may also notice the relationships you choose begin to change. You may feel drawn to people who communicate openly, who offer consistency, and who allow space for both closeness and individuality. You may become less comfortable in dynamics that rely on uncertainty, emotional distance, or constant reassurance.

Healthy connection often feels different than what you may have been used to. It may feel slower, steadier, and less intense at first. There may be fewer dramatic highs and fewer painful lows. Instead, connection develops through consistency, presence, and mutual understanding. This kind of connection may feel unfamiliar at first, but over time, it often becomes more grounding and sustainable.

As you continue forward, growth may become less about changing others and more about understanding yourself. You may recognize when you need reassurance, when you need space, or when you need to communicate more openly. These moments become opportunities to respond with awareness rather than reaction.

There is no final version of secure attachment, and no perfect way to love. There is only growth, awareness, and the ongoing process of learning. The way you learned to love shaped your past, but it does not have to define your future.

You adapted.

You survived.

You learned.

And now, you are allowed to love in ways that feel safer, calmer, and more authentic.

This does not mean you will never feel uncertain again. It does not mean relationships will always be easy. It means you move forward with greater awareness, greater compassion, and greater choice.

As you move forward, you are no longer confined by the defaults that once guided you. You are personalizing the settings — creating a way of loving that evolves with you, steady, intentional, and uniquely your own.

And perhaps that is the most meaningful shift of all.

You are no longer trying to become someone else.

You are simply becoming more fully yourself — and learning that love can finally feel safe.

ABOUT THE AUTHOR

Emily Elizabeth Hickman is a behavioral health therapist, writer, and transformational guide born and raised in the Appalachian Mountains of eastern Kentucky, where she continues to live today. Her work blends professional training with lived experience, focusing on helping individuals understand emotional patterns, navigate relationships, and move toward deeper self-awareness and healing.

Emily holds a Master's degree in Mental Health Counseling and brings a background in coaching, leadership, and human services to her work. She is particularly passionate about exploring how early experiences, attachment patterns, and family dynamics shape identity, relationships, and personal growth.

Her first book, *The Daughter I Had to Be*, explored shadow work, generational patterns, and the emotional adaptations we develop to survive. *The Space Between Replies* expands on those ideas, focusing on how attachment patterns shape the way we connect, communicate, and protect ourselves in relationships.

As a mother of two, a daughter and a son, Emily's work is deeply influenced by her commitment to generational healing and the belief that understanding ourselves more deeply allows us to show up differently for the people we love.

In addition to her nonfiction writing, Emily also writes poetry under the name Ember Evanesco Elderflower, exploring themes of healing, identity, grief, and transformation. Her poetry reflects the emotional undercurrents that shape both her writing and her work.

Emily continues to live and work in the Appalachian Mountains, where she supports others in understanding themselves more deeply and building healthier, more meaningful connections.

www.ingramcontent.com/pod-product-compliance
Lightning Source LLC
LaVergne TN
LVHW091139080826
845145LV00008B/2199

9781969649882